INVENT IT, SELL IT, BANK IT!

INVENT IT, SELL IT,
BANK IT!

MAKE YOUR
MILLION-
DOLLAR
IDEA
INTO A REALITY

Lori Greiner

BALLANTINE BOOKS
NEW YORK

Published in the United States by Ballantine Books, an imprint of Random House, a division of Random House LLC, a Penguin Random House Company, New York.

BALLANTINE and the HOUSE colophon are registered trademarks of Random House LLC.

Library of Congress Cataloging-in-Publication Data
Greiner, Lori.
Invent it, sell it, bank it! : make your million-dollar idea into a reality / Lori Greiner.
pages cm
ISBN 978-0-8041-7643-9 (hardback)—ISBN 978-0-8041-7644-6 (ebook)
1. Entrepreneurship. 2. Creative ability in business. I. Title.
HD53.G7454 2014
658.1'1—dc23
2014002157

Printed in the United States of America on acid-free paper

www.ballantinebooks.com

2 4 6 8 9 7 5 3 1

First Edition

Book design by Susan Turner

To my husband, Dan. You stood by me, loved me, and made me believe in myself. You have changed my life profoundly. I'll love you forever.

CONTENTS

"Do not go where the path may lead. Go instead where there is no path and leave a trail."

—RALPH WALDO EMERSON

In these pages you will find the story of my success, and the step-by-step path that I took to achieve my dreams. This is what worked for me, and the system detailed in these pages I hope helps you on your journey. But nothing in this life is guaranteed, and you may have different experiences along the way. Just remember, stay true to your vision and I wish you the very best of luck!

—*Lori*

INTRODUCTION

*"Every man-made thing, however small,
started in someone's imagination."*

—AUTHOR UNKNOWN

THE ALARM GOES OFF AT 4:30 A.M. I HATE EARLY MORNINGS. I'M a night owl, and if given my choice I go to sleep at 1 or 2 a.m. I drag myself out of bed, throw on jeans and a T-shirt—my get-to-the-set uniform—and still bleary-eyed manage to get myself to the Sony Pictures Studios lot, where *Shark Tank* is shot. It's the same set where *The Voice* is filmed. I'm the first shark to arrive at hair and makeup at 6:30 a.m. because I take the longest to get camera-ready—I have more hair than any of the other sharks! By 8:00 a.m. I'm dressed and made-up and downing my second huge cup of coffee, which I never drink except for when I'm shooting *Shark Tank*. It's going to be a long day, and I need to be sure that I'm completely alert. The other sharks trickle in. It's always good to see them and we joke around for a few minutes, but most of us are also on our phones, checking in with our respective businesses during the few moments of free time that we can squeeze in before shooting starts.

It's showtime. We settle in to our respective shiny red leather armchairs. We know nothing about what lies ahead. All we can see is a bare set, empty but for the colorful Persian-style carpet on the floor. Then the stagehands rush on with the props the first contestant will need to conduct his or her pitch. Loud, invigorating music is playing to pump us up and get everyone in a good mood to start the day. The stagehands disappear, and the director starts counting down. Five. Four. Three. Two. One. Quiet on the set! The large automatic doors in front of us swing open, and the first entrepreneur walks down the long hallway toward us, past the swimming sharks and into the tank.

There are about thirty seconds between the time new contestants walk through the double doors into the tank and the time they start their pitch. They stand on the carpet silently for a few seconds, facing the sharks, and then start their pitch. It's a nerve-wracking time for the entrepreneurs. They know this is their big moment. For the sharks, it represents a moment of anticipation.

I particularly notice which entrepreneurs make eye contact with me and which don't, as they stand there nervously. We see about eight or nine pitches per day. Last I heard, around 35,000 people applied to audition for a spot on Season Five. Each one who makes it onto the show is so hopeful, so eager to get a deal— not just for the influx of cash but also for the partnership, mentoring, and connections that any one of the five sharks can offer. As they talk, we furiously scribble down the financials, the retail history, and the valuations, to keep track of all the information coming at us. In the shadows, I know Dan, my husband, who is also the VP of my company, is sitting there writing everything down, too. All the sharks have someone on set who will typically take notes. We see many entrepreneurs a day, and though the TV audience sees only approximately twelve minutes of the pitch, the pitches can run anywhere from half an hour to two hours (that's unusually long, but it has happened). Because things go so fast and get so heated, I like reminders so I can recall in more detail everything that went on. I love reading the funny things the entrepreneurs or my fellow sharks have said. It's so interesting, and often hilarious, to look back a few weeks later when I'm reviewing my notes, and then to see it air on TV, when it comes to life all over again.

I work hard to make sure I give each pitch my full attention, especially the ones that show up last, when we are all exhausted. I concentrate, trying to ignore everything that might distract me— like the fact that it's often freezing because the air-conditioning is so strong. Nothing matters except the people standing there, pitching their hearts out in the hope that one of us will believe their idea is worth our investment of time, effort, and money.

It's a shame that viewers at home can't actually feel the crackle of energy that surges through the room when an inventor strikes a deal. It's so exciting to know that one of them will be on his or her way to a bigger journey! On the flip side, the entrepreneurs' disappointment is crushing when they leave the tank empty-handed. But for most of them, I think the disappointment is just temporary, for the true entrepreneurs live on and see promise in another day. That's their nature. I know the shark in me must be honest, not just because that's what's best for my business but also because that's what's best for the inventor's business, too. Dropping out or voicing concerns and criticism about the business or product being pitched is actually the kindest thing I could do. I'm doing someone a disservice if, out of pity or sympathy, I let an inventor get by with a product I truly think will never make it. I feel it's wiser to go back to the proverbial drawing board and try to create something new, something different, something better. Better to set your sights on the next product, something that really will work and allow you to reach the goals that inspire most inventors to start on their entrepreneurial journey—to strike out on their own, to build a career, to support a family, to leave a legacy. In short, to achieve the American Dream. I live that dream every day, and more than anything, I want to help others achieve it, too.

For years, fans of my show and products on QVC, followers on my website and social media networks, and *Shark Tank* supporters have been urging me to write a book. Many of them represent a fraction of the countless imaginative, creative individuals in this country who believe they have an idea that could be the next bendable straw, Q-tip, or George Foreman grill—a product so useful and practical that people might one day take its existence for granted. They usually want to know two things: how I got to where I am, and how they can get there, too. It's great to mentor up-and-coming inventors and share what I have learned over the last seventeen years about launching products and building a business from scratch, but when I think about what I did to bring that first invention to market, and all the products that followed, I realize that the answer to those two questions is quite simple: I worked hard. Really hard. That's what you have to do and how you become a successful inventor or entrepreneur: you work harder for it than you've ever worked at anything in your life.

Seventeen years ago, when I created my first product, an earring organizer, it was not because I wanted to run a multimillion-dollar conglomerate. I simply had a problem that I wanted to solve. But once I was sure I'd created the perfect solution, nothing was going to keep me from getting it onto the market so that I could help other women solve the problem, too. Whenever I hit a roadblock, I found a way around it. If I couldn't get around it, I went under it. If going under didn't work, I'd go over. I did whatever it took. In return, I accomplished my goal: I got my product prototyped, marketed, sold, manufactured, and on retailers' shelves in about four months. That is a difficult feat, but I was determined to make the holiday selling season. I wouldn't recommend trying to rush a product out in four months. Give yourself more time.

I'm ready to teach you what I know about everything from concept to creation, manufacturing to marketing, pitching, patents, and more, but you have to be willing to put in the long hours, the nights, the weekends, and most important, your heart and soul. I can show you the road, but those fundamentals— drive, determination, and red-hot passion—must be your fuel. Do you have that fire within you? Good! For anyone not scared off by that cornerstone piece of advice, read on. I've got plenty more, all of it in step-by-methodical-step, all of it self-taught, including this: while the work required to become a successful inventor is greater than you could ever imagine, it's more rewarding, too. The only regret you will ever have is that you didn't get started sooner.

Invent It, Sell It, Bank It! will tell you secrets about bringing products to market that you won't hear anywhere else. It includes checklists and tangible specifics you can use as your guide. It is a book about how you can make millions with your idea. You'll also find out how I did the same. I probably started out just like you. I had no experience running a business. I didn't have a ton of resources. I didn't know people in high places. I had a college degree, but I did not attend business school. In fact, I never even took a business class, my interests leaning more in a literary, cinematic, and artistic direction. Truly, I had no idea what I was doing. All I had was a great idea and the determination of twenty people put together to bring it to life. A brilliant idea doesn't guarantee a successful invention. Rather, it's a magical combination of a brilliant idea, plus amazing willpower, tenacity, and a willingness to make mistakes. Mistakes are good—and essential. They teach you to be better and smarter. But we'll get to that later.

I say I'm just like you, but inventors starting out today have many advantages that I didn't have. When I got started in 1996, there was no Internet where I could access information. There were no forums where I could network with other entrepreneurs. No Kickstarter or Indiegogo. There was definitely no *Shark Tank*. There were few resources available to help an inventor with no connections and a limited amount of capital. It was tough! So if I could turn my dream into reality, I know you can, too. You just have to want your dream as badly as I wanted mine.

It was 2008 when I got the call to come in and meet with Mark Burnett for a new show that he, ABC, and Sony were developing, called *Shark Tank*. The meeting went great and I was so excited to be chosen for the show. But then the most horrible thing happened: my mother, whom I loved very much, died suddenly right at the same time as shooting, and I had to withdraw. It was a difficult time. The producers kept in touch with me, and three years later, I appeared in Season Three as a guest shark, and then I became a permanent shark in Season Four.

Early on, the casting agent shared with me one of the reasons the show's creators had sought me out. She said I was a unicorn; there just wasn't anyone else out there like me. I had never thought about it. Many inventors can point to one phenomenally successful product, but it's rarer for someone to bring a large number of inventions to market. I've developed over four hundred successful products, and I have a hundred and twenty patents. People are always asking me if I'm proud of that, and I am. But what gives me the greatest pleasure is having created so many products that make people happy and make their lives easier. Had I stopped after witnessing the success of my first invention, I would have been proud of that, too. It's not about the number of inventions you bring to market. Margaret Mitchell published only one novel, but it was *Gone with the Wind!* There is great satisfaction in developing one fantastic product and watching the world fall in love with it. And it only takes the successful launch of one brilliant idea to make you a millionaire. But whether you create one great thing or many, the steps to get you there are the same.

Why didn't I stop at one invention? For the same reason many entrepreneurs keep churning away even after their business takes off—the sheer joy of it. Besides, once you've brought one successful product to market, you know everything you need to bring another successful product to market. If anything, success only makes you want to work harder. When you are as obsessed and determined as most inventors who have built thriving, lucrative businesses, work doesn't feel like work. It feels like freedom. Inventors and entrepreneurs constitute a special club, a collection of creative spirits and mavericks who simply can't or won't conform to the established boundaries and limitations of the traditional workplace.

We are the kind of people who must forge our own paths, not follow one already laid out for us. Like everyone else, we want to make money, but we want to earn it doing something that we love and that we can call our own. We choose to whittle our lives down to the bare essentials—family, food, sleep—because we know that every hour of effort we put in will come directly back to us and to the people we love. It may seem to outsiders like a Spartan life, all work and no play, but it isn't, because when you're doing what you love, work is play. They will never understand what a powerful thrill it is to hold in your hands something you dreamed up in your head.

That said, my philosophy is that life's a party and you've got to have fun every day. I believe that there's always room for good food, wine, and laughter, whether it's just Dan and me going over numbers together late at night or

> "Entrepreneurship is living a few years of your life like most people won't so you can spend the rest of your life like most people can't."
> —AUTHOR UNKNOWN

my whole team gathered for last-minute preparations for a show. Even when you're working, you should be having a good time!

One more thing that sets me apart from many other inventors and entrepreneurs is that I preach extreme DIY. My expertise doesn't come from the sheer number of products I can list; it's a result of being directly involved in every facet of their creation. There is nothing you cannot learn yourself. Who can you trust better than yourself to get things done right? No one will ever care as much as you do about your business.

You don't know about manufacturing? Neither did I, but now I could run a factory if I needed to. You aren't a lawyer and don't know a thing about patents? I'm not either, but now I'm educated to the point that I help write my patents, and I've been called as a guest speaker for the U.S. Patent and Trade Office in Washington, D.C. There was a time when I didn't know anything about what it took to bring a product to market, but I figured it out. The stories you'll read in this book will reveal the lengths to which I was willing to go to ensure my products' success, and that it would offer both value and pleasure to anyone who bought them. As my business grew larger, I would eventually have to delegate some responsibilities, but in those early days I insisted on being there for every step. What I didn't know, I'd learn. If I wasn't an expert, I'd become one. No detail was too small, and my efforts paid off. Because in the end, all you've got is what you're willing to bring, so you'd better bring it all!

As in all things, natural creative talent will get you only so far. If you want to see your invention on shelves, in stores, on television, and most important, in people's hands and homes, you have to develop skills to support your talent. To become a successful inventor, it's not enough to have a great idea for a product. You have to design it and manufacture it. You have to protect your design from being copied or stolen. You have to package your product and pitch it. You have to find someone willing to sell it. All of those steps require skills and finesse that you can often only learn on the job.

Lucky for you, I already have. In *Invent It, Sell it, Bank It!* you will learn about the ins and outs of great product design, from concept to creation; the nuts and bolts of manufacturing, patenting, packaging, pricing, and shipping; the art of the pitch, the trick to inexpensive yet effective marketing, the rules and regulations that must be followed, and the key to lining up multiple retail sources.

I'm excited to share everything I know and to give you an honest and straightforward overview of what it takes to get a product to market. It's not always an easy road. Like everyone else I've had my fair share of hard knocks in life. I think that's good. Struggles and setbacks make you stronger and better. And most of the time what you think is the worst thing that could happen to you turns out to be a blessing in disguise. Every time something goes wrong, you will learn from it and become better able to cope with the next challenge or obstacle that comes your way.

To all budding entrepreneurs I say this: you can make almost anything happen if you try hard enough. When you run your own business, you're taking a different journey than the average person. You're embarking on a 24/7 commitment. You never really shut the door. You'll take vacations, but things will come up and you have to be available. You need to support your team. You'll need a lot of energy to succeed in this business. You have to dream bigger. You have to reach further. I am living proof that, with enough fire and willpower, you can make anything happen. Failure is not an option; it's a state of mind.

This book outlines the invention process in linear fashion— first you do this, then you do that. But realize that when you're bringing a product to market, you're doing everything at once. When I launched my first invention, I ran around like a nut. It was summer and I wanted my product out for the holiday season, which meant I had to make a miracle happen. I had every fire going at the same time. While my prototype was being made, I was calling stores and pitching my idea. Once the prototype was done, I continued to make calls while at the same time conducting market research. Next thing I knew, I was flying around the country making my pitch, visiting stores from Chicago to Minneapolis to Texas to California, ultimately traveling to nineteen cities in twenty-one days! At the same time, I continued to call other stores, working on tooling, designing my packaging, and selecting a factory. I worked my butt off, and thankfully I made a miracle happen. And I've continued to work that way ever since. The thing is, that's the way most people who achieve success in this business do things. I hope that my story will be inspiring, and that getting a peek into my thought process will be helpful when it's time for you to start making your own rapid-fire decisions.

Invent It, Sell It, Bank It! will reveal how I mastered strategic and technical skills, but it may also explain why I have become known as "the warm-blooded shark" on *Shark Tank*. I don't think being kind or compassionate makes me any less competitive in the business world. I see no point in tearing people down to get ahead, and I have also found that you can never go wrong if you try to be nice. That's why I do my best to be respectful to all the entrepreneurs who come into the tank—even the ones whose businesses in my opinion don't show much promise. When I look at them, I see myself. I know what it is like to have one shot that could make or break everything. I've been in their shoes. I remember the people who let me down nicely, and those who treated me brutally. It brings to mind something my grandfather always told me: people will forget what you said, they will forget what you did, but they will never forget how you made them feel. I'm far from perfect, but I always try to remember his words. I've never believed I had to be cutthroat or cruel to get ahead in business. However, never mistake my kindness for weakness.

It's a paradox: you are responsible for your own destiny, but you can't get there alone. No matter how sure you are that you know what's best for your product, no matter how high your standards, it's important to be kind to people and to make them feel a part of a team. Take the time to invest in people, not just your product. The height or longevity of any success you achieve will correlate with how well you nurture your relationships with the people who cross your path along the way. You can be kind and compassionate and still be a shark. You'll be amazed at how far that combination will get you, especially when you're armed with all the information you need to bring your dream to reality.

How do I know this is true? Every move I make on *Shark Tank,* and every negotiation I engage in with the contestants or even with the other sharks, is informed by years of lessons learned the hard way. *Shark Tank* is merely an extension of what I've been doing throughout my career. While I did spend the majority of time creating, patenting, and manufacturing my own products, I always enjoyed helping others along the way. And with this book, I have the opportunity to reach even more, and to offer my take on the ins and outs of the inventor's world in more depth and

> "Entrepreneurs: the only people who work eighty hours a week to avoid working forty hours a week."
>
> —Author Unknown

detail than ever before. Finally, with *Invent It, Sell It, Bank It!* I can share everything I've learned over the past seventeen years of inventing products and running a business with anyone who's seen me in the tank, my other habitat, QVC, or in retail stores. But of course this book isn't just for fans of these shows. Anyone with a creative spirit, tremendous drive, and a terrific idea can use it to invent his or her own way to wealth and success. My number one rule has always been to make great products that help people. I hope this book helps you.

INVENT IT, SELL IT, BANK IT!

1

ARE YOU READY?

"Every accomplishment starts with the decision to try."
—GAIL DEVERS, three-time Olympic champion in track and field

WHEN WE THINK ABOUT THE WORLD'S GREATEST INVENTORS, we tend to remember a select few whose innovations quite literally changed the world. Thomas Edison for the phonograph and the first incandescent lightbulb that was safe and practical enough for home use; Nikola Tesla or Guglielmo Marconi, depending whom you ask, for the radio; George Washington Carver, for peanut butter; Wilbur and Orville Wright, for the airplane. And yet, every day we take advantage of products and devices created by millions of inventors who are not and may never be household names, but who have made our world a better place. They are young, like Chester Greenwood, who invented the earmuff when he was only fifteen, and they are old, like Charles Greeley Abbot, who invented the first solar cooker and was 101 when he received his last patent. They are moms—notorious for creating new time and labor-saving devices, including the disposable diaper—and dads, like Frank Epperson, inventor of the Popsicle (originally called the Eppsicle). They are tinkerers who constantly take things apart to see how they work, only to immediately identify how they could build them better; troubleshooters who get energized when hunting for creative solutions to life's everyday dilemmas; and DIYers whose impatience with inefficiency or disorganization leads to jerry-rigged home storage solutions and ingenious contraptions that leave their friends agape with admiration and begging for their own.

TRULY, ANYONE, AT ANY TIME, can become an inventor. And yet, the numbers are sobering. Out of all the patents that are filed every year in the United States, only about 1 percent are for products that actually get made and reach the market. In addition, Richard Maulsby, former director of public affairs for the U.S. Patent and Trademark Office, told *Bloomberg Business Week* that, "It's a very small percentage of patents that actually turn into products that make money for people." But it does happen, sometimes in spectacular fashion. So the question is, how do millionaire inventors beat the odds and achieve commercial success—and how can you join their ranks?

That is why you picked up this book, isn't it? You want to know how they did it? How I did it? Though the details of everyone's story are different, there are often common themes. A spectacular, often simple idea. Hard work. Good timing. And yet, research suggests that the seeds to successful inventions are often sown in an inventor's character, long before he or she ever has the brilliant idea that required such good timing and hard work to strike gold. Psychological profiles of famously prolific inventors and entrepreneurs like Martha Stewart and Richard Branson reveal that most share certain strengths and characteristics. Before

I became an inventor, none of my interests or ambitions would have predicted that I'd wind up on the entrepreneurial path, and yet as it turns out I do fit the mold and possess most of these character traits. I think that explains why it was actually fun for me, not frightening, to maneuver around the obstacles that confronted me when I was trying to bring my first idea to market, and to ensure that the odds were better than average that my inventions could become the foundation of an exciting and lucrative career.

You're probably feeling something burn inside, a powerful force that insists this is your destiny, too. That's a good sign. But it's not enough. I'm not saying you're confusing heartburn with a hunger for success; I'm just cautioning you that the road to successful invention is not easy, and sometimes we too easily dismiss or ignore our weaknesses. For an inventor, that's a dangerous thing. It's important that you know yourself well before taking one more step. You can be a source of truly spectacular ideas, but ideas without follow-through go nowhere; determination untempered by a willingness to face reality can lead to bankruptcy; dreams unsupported by strong stamina and organizational skills tend to die. But if after deep self-reflection you are still convinced that you do possess a solid number of the following character traits and tendencies, you can move forward knowing that you're starting out with the right stuff.

THE SIX ESSENTIAL CHARACTERISTICS OF SUCCESSFUL INVENTORS

Passion

If there's one thing that unites all inventors, regardless of who they are or whom they are selling to, it's their passion for their inventions. I treat each one of mine like my babies, including ones I didn't actually invent but invested in. One of my colleagues at

QVC used to joke that I could sell mud—that's how strongly I believe in my products and how infectious is my enthusiasm. Actually, that's how strongly I believe in most things that are important to me. I don't know how to dabble. I'm either going to jump into something wholeheartedly and for the long haul, or I'm just not interested at all. So whatever product I fall in love with, or whatever business I champion, I'm behind it 100 percent! And since I fall in love with most of the products I create or businesses I support, it's just not that hard to get everyone else who matters behind them 100 percent, too. And as you'll see, once you get the people who matter to support you and your idea, you're halfway to seeing your dream become a million-dollar reality.

> Passion is a
> powerful sales tool.
> When combined
> with hard evidence,
> it is irresistible.

I've never met a single inventor who was lackadaisical about his or her creation. Inventors' descriptions can even be overexaggerations: "My money-dispensing, hot-chocolate making, floating skateboard is the most important advancement in transportation since Henry Ford's Model T!" Later, we'll discuss how to objectively determine whether your invention deserves that kind of hype, but for now, your enthusiasm for and belief in your idea really should be that intense. You're going to need that degree of passion to sustain you through the incredible journey you will take as you shepherd your invention from concept to commercial—and lucrative—stardom.

However, make sure you're passionate about the right things. A lot of entrepreneurs and inventors are passionate about making money, but you don't start your journey with the goal of becoming a millionaire. It won't work. No one gets rich merely because he or she wants to get rich. You get rich because you bring something into the world that is unique and that people are willing to pay for. You get rich when you can successfully prove to others how amazing your product or service is. You can sell a million dollars' worth of goods, but if a million dollars' worth of goods are returned, you've accomplished nothing. When I started out, of course I hoped I'd make money, but it was the art of perfecting my product, and the excitement of launching the business, that drove me. Start with the important part: create something special. Believe in it so much that other people can't help but see it the way you see it. Do that right, and the money will follow.

Confidence

You will get nowhere if you carry around the idea that you are less important or less deserving of success than anyone else. The inventor's arena is no place for self-doubt. You need to believe in yourself as passionately as you believe in your product. You will encounter plenty of people who will be looking for reasons to say no, or to make you feel as though you are not worthy of their respect and consideration. Do not let them, regardless of whether they have more clout, better educations, bigger reputations, or fancy nameplates. Your success will have everything to do with how you perceive yourself, because how you perceive yourself is how others will perceive you, too.

That's a message for everyone, men and women alike. But an important note to women: don't ever think of yourself as a woman in business. Rather, think of yourself as a businessperson, equal to anyone else and better than some depending on the areas of your expertise. That's how I see myself. Aside from giving me firsthand insight into the female consumer's mind, being a woman has had no bearing on how I do business. I think that's why it's always been such a shock when I've found myself face-to-face with sexism. The first patent lawyer I ever met with was a man in his thirties who had somehow never heard of the women's movement.

My husband, Dan, accompanied me to our first meeting because he was interested in hearing what the attorney had to say, since any decisions I made would necessarily affect his finances, too—I used our money, about $5,000, to pay for the first patent filing. I sat across from the lawyer so we could face each other, and Dan purposely sat off to the side as a listener, not a participant. He remained silent as I talked, and yet every time I would ask a question, the attorney would turn to my husband to reply. I was shocked at how blatant this was, but he went on, oblivious to what he was doing. I kept asking questions to see how long he was going to continue this way. He went on and kept directing his replies to Dan. After about ten minutes, I said, "Okay. I'm done. I'd appreciate if you would go find one of the partners of this firm. Tell them you have been such a chauvinist to me that they need to send in a female attorney to help me instead of you." Maybe that was reverse chauvinism, but I didn't want to risk this happening again, and I felt I could avoid it for sure by asking to work with a woman. The attorney blushed and stammered and tried to say he was sorry, but I wasn't interested in his apology. "You're not really sorry. You're only sorry that I called you on it." Fortunately, the lawyer who replaced him, Natalie, is a terrific attorney. Seventeen years and 120 patents later,

Call out injustice when you see it, and always stand up for yourself. But be polite even as you do it— you'll get a lot further when you gain a reputation for taking the high ground.

I'm still with her to this day, and I consider her a dear friend. I'm so glad that guy screwed up. It just goes to show that things happen for a reason.

I've been asked if I'm ever nervous when I go head to head with fellow sharks Mark Cuban or Kevin O'Leary on *Shark Tank*. On the contrary, I like sparring with them. And besides, why would I feel nervous? Because Mark is a billionaire? Because Kevin is ruthless and has an acid-tipped tongue? They're unbelievably smart, they have worked extraordinarily hard and made brilliant business decisions, and they run tremendous empires— they deserve respect. But does that mean I can't stand up to them? Does it mean they are better than me, or anyone else? Of course not. They are just admirable and very successful. We are all just human beings in the end. I have my areas of expertise and they have theirs. And boy, do we all have our opinions!

I have my parents to thank for the mindset that I can achieve anything I want to. I have a tendency to be fearless in business (though you won't catch me within 10 yards of an iguana) and it has served me well. For any challenging situation, my father would say, "Think about what's the worst thing that can happen." So I'd think about it. Once I knew what the worst thing was, I'd say, "Okay, I can deal with that," and move forward. If I couldn't deal with it, I'd go in a different direction. When I went to start the business, once again I thought, "What's the worst that can happen?" In the early days I'd worry that a new product wouldn't be a hit, and that all the time and effort that went into it would have been for nothing. I had good instincts, but not a crystal ball. What if this time the product flopped? Then I'd force myself to get some perspective, and realize that a flopped product wasn't the end of the world.

Disappointing? Frustrating? Yes. Catastrophic? No. I had a plan in place should the worst ever happen. I think it's the fear of the bad things that can happen that stalls people and makes them freeze. If you can conceive of the worst, and you're prepared to deal with it, should you get there, everything else that comes before it is pretty manageable. It's good to have a plan, but don't be too rigid. Rigidity stifles creativity and keeps you from zigging and zagging when necessary. Things come up, and you'll have to go with the flow.

Some things are out of your control, such as when a buyer could make an arbitrary decision that would affect the future of your product. I've been fortunate in that the majority of people I've worked with, from retail buyers to attorneys to manufacturers, genuinely want the inventors and business owners with whom they do business to succeed. But eventually, you're going to run into someone who is having a really bad day and decides to take it out on you. There will be nothing you can do about that. It's your attitude that will matter, and how you deal with these people. At the end of the day, if someone proves impossible to work with, find someone else. If something doesn't go in your favor, try something else. It's never one thing or nothing; there's always a way. Having confidence will protect you and get you through those moments.

Just don't allow your confidence to slide into arrogance or rudeness. There's no excuse for either. I've seen many new inventors lose lucrative deals because they were so smug, were inflexible, or carried themselves with such a sense of entitlement that no one wanted to do business with them. I walked away from one of the best products I've ever seen because its creator was such a know-it-all, and so convinced he had nothing to learn, that he never heard anything anyone had to say. For me, no amount of money is ever worth the headache of having to deal with someone like that. I want to enjoy my business partners and do great business together, not fight with them. That's not to say inventors shouldn't stand up for what they believe, even if it means disagreeing with their investors or buyers. If you have a point, make it, but always do so respectfully and with an explanation. Being a good leader is being a good listener. Be the person who others want to have on their team, to buy from, or to work with. Remember, buyers are judged by how well their product lines sell. If you work as a team and acknowledge their contributions, your success can be their success, too, and they'll enjoy working with you.

Confidence is also what will give you the strength you need to ignore skeptics. There will be many. Some may be jealous, or threatened, or simply unimaginative. Others may genuinely have your best interest at heart. They care about you and they're scared that you'll fail. And that's why they are the skeptics and you're the entrepreneur—because you don't approach life with fear, but with courage; you prefer to take the positive angle rather than the negative one. If someone doesn't believe in your idea, it's typically because the person has never seen it before or couldn't make it work. When others say, "What if this doesn't work?" your attitude should be, "It will work when I figure out how to make it work." When they say, "That's never been done," your answer should be, "That's the point."

Drive and Determination

You have to have incredible amounts of these two. Drive is your inner momentum, that insatiable need inventors have, as powerful and primal as hunger or thirst, to keep working and moving toward their goals. Determination is your will, your conscious decision to set those goals, commit to achieving them, and then set more once you've achieved the first ones. Your drive fuels your determination, and determination is what helps you override symptoms like stress or fatigue that can weaken your resolve to persevere. Drive and determination manifest themselves in your willingness to do the work of twenty, if necessary.

Successful inventors generally don't know how to sit still, nor would they want to. Where's the fun in that? The additional advantage to being so highly determined and having loads of drive is that once you've invested all that energy and work into getting your product to market, you will know everything that needs to be done. If you've been as hands-on as most successful inventors usually are, you've learned the tricks and the traps, become familiar with the laws and the regulations. You've seen the ugly and dodged the bullets, negotiated opportunities and reeled in the deals. With that experience under your belt, it's much easier to get your second product off the ground. And even easier to launch your third. Of course, there will always be surprises, but they become fewer and farther between.

Organizational Skills

I believe that when you've got a great idea, you should move as fast as possible to get it to market. I often say that I don't let the grass grow under my feet. Neither should you. When you've got a terrific idea and you can't wait to get it off the ground, it's to your advantage to try getting as many balls in motion as possible.

However, be careful. Sometimes people compose a grand business plan, complete with financial projections, when they haven't yet calculated how much it's going to cost them to make their product. How could their financial plan be viable? It's important to see the big picture, of course, but your ability to appreciate the details and recognize square one is essential. For the record, square one is always this: accurately identifying and describing your product, followed up by figuring out how you're going to make it, and what it's going to cost. These are the basics. Everything that happens next, from the research you undertake to the connections you try to make, will stem from your answers to those initial questions. And for every hoop you jump through on your way to achieving your goals, three more hoops will materialize. There's always one more form to fill out, one more phone call to make, one more person to track down. So you'll need to have discipline and an organized system to keep on task.

Many of today's inventors probably rely on any number of apps for that. My system, however, has always been and remains quite low tech. I keep lists on my iPhone and computer, but my team teases me about the number of yellow notepads I have. I love notepads. I love writing things down with an inky pen and seeing the scope of my to-do's all in front of me at one time so I can prioritize. I have a lot of balls in the air at one time and the list changes frequently. I'll write five columns on the front page listing all my *Shark Tank* ventures; my QVC business; contracts, agreements, and negotiations; new product development; outside retailers; video shoots; social media, and more. I try to check things off as I go through them, but it's always a work in progress. Then I rewrite my lists to narrow them down, and of course they instantly get just as crowded again. I usually have about four notepads going at any one time, and then when I travel I condense them down to two. It sounds crazy to schlep all that weight in this day of sleek phones and wafer-thin computers and tablets, but nothing beats the satisfaction of writing on a lined piece of paper with a black pen, and then crossing the words out. That quirk probably helps explain why I'm drawn to inventing tactile products and not techy ones.

It's hard for entrepreneurs to delegate, but over time I've learned how. And yet my to-do lists remain as long as ever because I stay so closely involved with each of my products, projects, and ventures. I can ask people to communicate with our factories, and trust others to arrange for samples to be shipped on time or transmit orders, but only I can confirm that a product's design and creation are true to my vision.

One last thing should be said about being organized and making plans. Of course, you need to make them, but a smart entrepreneur also knows when to go off script. It's common for people to believe that before they embark on a big project they need to have a fully outlined master plan. I've never worked that way; I don't think it's wise. How can you make a plan when you don't even know where to begin? Only by figuring out each step you need to take can you see the shape of your plan. Each discovery leads to the next one, so your plans will always need to adapt. Figure out what you're going to need next, and then use your organizational skills to get to that next step. Allow yourself room to be spontaneous, to change your mind or adjust your expectations. Structure and discipline are important, but don't ever let your plan become a cage that bars you from reacting quickly, taking advantage of opportunities, or adapting to new realities. Be willing to change tactics midstream if that's what it takes to solve a problem and get you to your end game.

Though many of my products are intended to help make people's lives easier or better, and several of them have been organizers, I'm not freakishly organized. I do believe, however, that chaos, clutter, and disorganization make you crabby and your day harder. I know it did for my mom. The home where I grew up was neat and orderly, except for my mother's bedroom. She worked, she was busy, and she was always running late. I have strong memories of watching her scramble around, hunting frantically for some misplaced earring, lipstick, or shoe. I was very close to my mother growing up. She'd spend thirty minutes searching for something like her lipstick—"My lipstick. Where's my red lipstick?"—and I'd walk in and immediately pick it up from her nightstand. "You mean this one?" We'd crack up.

It happened all the time. Who knows, maybe watching my mom taught me that life goes just a little more smoothly when things are put away where they belong, and that means having a place to put them. When I started inventing products, I tried to think of things that people needed and wanted. There are so many things in life that we cannot control, but our stuff doesn't have to be one of them! I design a lot of organizers because it makes people's lives easier, including my own. My mom owned every single one of them. In fact, she owned every single thing I ever made, and watched every show I was ever on, calling me to share her thoughts after every one. Of course, she loved everything—she was my mom.

My mom's nemesis was her cluttered bedroom; mine is my office. It's a nightmare, and I have yet to invent or find any tool to help me tame it. Like a lot of people, as soon as I put papers away, I forget about them, so I have to leave them scattered all over my desk. It's chaos. When you're a busy person (and who isn't?), stuff just winds up everywhere. One of these days I hope I'll come up with a solution for the office. Or I hope *you* will.

Self-Sufficiency and Independence

You'd think that it would go without saying that an inventor needs to be self-sufficient, but based on the questions people ask me, it does need to be said. I think some people believe that because they have an independent streak, they are naturally self-sufficient, too. But that's not always the case. I've lost count of the number of entrepreneurs who have asked me for information, and after I've given them some guidelines about how to research their question, have come back at me with, "Couldn't you just tell me what to do?" I don't think those people stand a chance. You may want to be your own boss, but if you don't have the wherewithal to figure it out on your own, you won't make it.

One of the hardest things about being an entrepreneur is that there is no one around to tell you what to do, and no one to make sure you do it. That's what I love about it, but for others I often wonder, how will they cope? I'm sure they understand, rationally, what it means to be self-employed, but many will find it surprisingly hard to stick to a self-imposed regimen. You've got to be the kind of person who doesn't need direction and enjoys figuring things out for yourself. My husband always jokes that I can never do anything like everyone else. They will be driving in one lane; I'm always off creating my own. Being independent doesn't mean, of course, that you shouldn't turn to others for expertise or guidance. It's a wise person who knows how and when to do that. But you must have the initiative to take whatever you learn and run with it. Ultimately, it will make you a stronger, more competitive businessperson to try to figure things out on your own. Your mistakes will be all yours, but so will your triumphs.

Charisma and Showmanship

The three years you spent holed up alone in your garage tinkering with your product may have been the happiest days of your life, but they will be wasted and your invention will never see the light of day if you are afraid to talk to strangers about it. People drawn to entrepreneurialism are typically outgoing and unafraid of making public speeches, but I've often heard protests along the lines of, "I'm a scientist/engineer/accountant, not a salesperson." It's fine to live a life of the mind while building your invention, but if you ever want to sell it, you'll need to embrace the limelight, too. Shyness will sink you in this business.

We've discussed the importance of passion, and here, too, it plays a role. A large part of successful selling is demonstrating tremendous passion for your product or idea, because enthusiasm and excitement is infectious. But in general, the best salespeople do genuinely like people. They like getting to know others and developing rapport, and most of all, they know how to listen so they can learn what people want or need. Developing charm (yes, it can be learned), being sensitive to others, and feeling at ease around strangers can be a challenge if you're naturally shy, but it's critical that you be able to draw people in and read them well, even if you've only got a few seconds with them, so that you can tailor your pitch accordingly. There's also a bit of showmanship required for great selling, so if you suffer from stage fright, now is the time to start working on beating it back. Acting classes, comedy classes, public speaking courses, and especially improv classes are great training grounds for introverts and others who want to sharpen their communication and presentation skills.

If you've done everything you can to improve your salesman-ship, but you still don't feel that you can represent your product the way it deserves, this is one of the few instances in which it would be not just acceptable but also imperative to bring in someone else with better people skills to do your presentations and pitches for you. You'll probably hate that bit of advice. How could I suggest that you trust someone else with your baby, someone who couldn't possibly care about it as much as you do? I'm telling you, if public speaking is really a struggle for you, you have to do it. It's the only way you're going to get anyone to pay attention.

Finally, if your business is large enough, you could ask an employee to pitch for you, or you could hire an outside sales rep or distributor. We'll talk more about how those business arrange-ments work and their advantages when we get to the art of the pitch in Chapter 7.

One Last, Important Thing . . .

Although it is not a character trait, there is one other thing a successful inventor needs, and I would be remiss not to mention it here: money. All the passion, confidence, drive, determination, charisma, and showmanship in the world will not help you if you don't have enough money to pay for the bare necessities, such as a prototype and travel expenses so you can meet with buyers and show your product. In addition, count on everything costing more than you think it will. There are many inspiring stories of people down to their last dimes whose inventions saved their families from financial ruin and went on to make millions. There are many more who spent everything they had on their inventions and were left with nothing to show for their efforts. This book is filled with advice that should help you avoid that kind of disaster, but nothing can change the fact that invention is still a risky business. Be prepared. We'll discuss where, when, and how to pursue funding options in more detail in Chapter 5.

A SUCCESSFUL INVENTOR DOESN'T NEED . . .

A Business Background

Many inventors are extremely entrepreneurial and business-savvy, the types who knew they were going to create their own business from the time they learned to tie their shoes. They start selling glow sticks to schoolmates at the age of nine and are working on their third business plan by the time they are in their early twenties. I was not really that person. In retrospect, however, I can definitely see that I had an inventor's brain, which is a lot like one of those spinning-wheel fireworks, the kind that shoots flames and sparks as it rotates in a pyrotechnic whirl of color and light; the kind that once it catches fire, there's no stopping (you're probably nodding your head in recognition).

But though my mind was constantly spinning with ideas, there is little in my background to suggest that I would become an inventor and entrepreneur. I studied television, journalism, and film.

I gave up my journalistic ambitions because I thought I might like to make movies, and I also dreamed of being a Tony Award–winning playwright. I handcrafted my own jewelry and I never, ever read the business section of the paper. You really never met a less business-y type than me. If that sounds like you, take heart—a business background can be helpful to inventors, but you don't need it.

Overhead

I'm amazed at how many people feel that they need to make a good impression by putting themselves up in a sharp-looking suite in a cool part of town. What for? Who's going to see your office when you're the one who's going to travel for meetings? Avoid spending money unless you absolutely have to. Try to work out of your home for as long as you can, even if you have a few employees, to keep overhead low. If you need storage, you can hire fulfillment centers that will store your product, and even put labels on it before shipping it out, or sometimes you can negotiate assembly and shipping straight from the manufacturer.

Many new inventors come on *Shark Tank* asking for thousands of dollars because they feel they need to hire staff. More often than not, they don't. If you eventually need a specialist like a graphic designer, you can hire a freelancer who will work out of his or her own space, not yours. You can answer your own phone or get an automated system. You can keep track of your own books. You have to be willing to do as much as possible by yourself up until you simply have no choice but to hire someone; and even then, you will have to stay intimately involved in the day-to-day operations, because even the best employee will never be as vigilant as you will.

You will make so much more money if you remain frugal even when your invention starts to succeed and your business begins to grow. For now and for the near future, enjoy roughing it. Take pride in the fact that you're tough enough to run a business on a tight budget. There will be plenty of time later to indulge in luxuries, comforts, and labor-saving purchases, and you'll appreciate them more. I was in business for four years before I finally indulged in my first big celebratory purchase—a stainless steel Cartier watch that I still love to this day. Sally, a supplier in London, and I had worked exceedingly hard on selling a product for QVC, and the channel had chosen it to be a "Today's Special Value," which is when they order a huge number of units and try to sell the entire amount in one day at a special low cost to the customer. We sold out. It was a huge milestone to get a TSV and sell it out in one day. Sally and I were ecstatic.

The next time I was in London, Sally and I met at Harrods for lunch, and of course we found ourselves in the massive jewelry hall looking at the gorgeous watches. Spontaneously, we decided we should buy ourselves something to remember this important occasion always. We both bought far more expensive watches than we ever had before. Whenever I look at that watch I remember that momentous occasion. It is one of both of our fondest memories.

To Be Unwilling to Accept Failure

This one comes as a big surprise for many inventors. But in fact, it's the inventors who refuse to accept failure that actually fail. It's one thing to ignore skeptics; it's another to ignore when every person you talk to—including the important ones, those with experience in the field who judge products every day—consistently tells you that your idea just isn't going to work. It is not failure, however, to accept that the idea isn't working, and move on to another one. It's smart. Know when to move on. Moving on is not the same thing as giving up. It's

> "Courage does not always roar. Sometimes courage is the quiet voice at the end of the day saying, I will try again tomorrow."
>
> –MARY ANNE RADMACHER

about refocusing your energy toward the next great thing you're going to accomplish. Besides, sometimes what looks like failure is often an important milestone on the path to achievement.

REMEMBER TO HAVE FUN

If you're interested in more comprehensive analyses of what makes a great inventor, or you want to see how you compare to entrepreneurial superstars, there are many books and diagnostics available. One of my favorites is *Entrepreneurial Genius*, by Gene Landrum. But in the end, all you can do is try. You'll know soon enough if you're not cut out for this life. Just remember that it's supposed to be fun. When I finally gave in and devoted myself full time to my products, I didn't mind that I was working every night and weekend. I didn't mind all the exhausting travel. I had my husband by my side encouraging me, and wherever I went I made sure to try to have a little fun by going to a great restaurant or seeing some sights before hopping back on the plane to Chicago. I was always designing, planning, plotting, and making lists in my head. I found each day exciting and invigorating because I knew all my efforts were coming back to me.

On the flip side, I was too naïve to know that it was going to be such a long road ahead, what I'd have to tackle, and what comes with starting a business and maintaining it. If it's anxiety instead of excitement keeping you up at night, you'll want to reconsider your decision to take this path. Pursuing a dream is admirable, but to do it at the expense of your health, your family, your financial well-being, and even your sanity is not good. Life is just too short to spend it doing something you don't enjoy.

If you embody all the characteristics in this chapter, and you can't imagine anything more fun than spending every waking minute tending to your invention, keep at it. Set your goals and attain them. Don't let fear of failure or hardships get in your way. There is always going to be something that doesn't go right. Glitches happen; that's the nature of the business. It's how you deal with them that will make the difference. Fear stems from the unknown. But if you know that whatever problems occur you're prepared to fix them, what's there to be afraid of? If you're vigilant, then you know you are going to spot glitches or problems as they come down the pike before they become insurmountable. Always do the right thing, and if you're committed to doing that, you have no reason to fear.

You've got an amazing idea for a product that is going to take the world by storm, and you can't wait to get it into as many hands as possible. You're bursting with creative energy. You know deep in your bones that you've got the fire, the tenacity, and the temperament to successfully fulfill your ambition. So go for it. There's never been a better time to turn your big idea into a big success.

KEEP IN MIND:

- Anyone can have the next big idea; not just anyone can bring it to fruition.
- You must be independent, organized, and willing to take risks.
- You will have a better chance at success when you approach challenges from a positive angle.
- Your worst enemy is self-doubt. Never underestimate or undervalue yourself.
- Keep a clear view of your strengths and weaknesses.
- Entrepreneurialism is supposed to be fun!

2

IS YOUR IDEA A HERO OR A ZERO?

*"Sometimes the smallest step in the right direction
ends up being the biggest step of your life.
Tip-toe if you must, but take the first step."*

—AUTHOR UNKNOWN

- A tiny magnet that keeps your glasses attached to your shirt even when you're doing a somersault: Yes
- Removable full-face tattoos for avid sports fans who want to show their team spirit without the effort and mess of face paint: Yes
- A cotton shower cap-style head covering to keep cooking odors out of your hair: No
- A squirrel-proof birdfeeder that delivers an electric shock to hungry squirrels via remote control: Heck no

MY BUSINESS INSTINCTS ARE POWERFUL AND RELIABLE. I MAY not be able to calculate profit percentages or compound interest formulas rapidly off the top of my head, but I can look at any product, such as the ones listed above, and instantly know if it's a hero or a zero. But here's the thing about instincts: they don't come out of thin air. Every time I instantaneously assess a product—mine or anyone else's—I'm also subconsciously running through a series of questions in my mind.

I've always had a strong awareness of what sells and why people buy, which enables me to answer these in just a few seconds—so fast that I'm not even aware I'm doing it. I feel fortunate to have this gift. Yet the speed with which one can answer these questions is not important. What's important is that they get asked and answered, period. The answers will tell you whether your idea is as commercially viable as you believe it is. If you want to break into the market, you've got to be willing to mercilessly scrutinize your product and open yourself up to brutally honest, objective judgment. If you can do that—without fudging, and without offering justifications or excuses when your answers aren't what you'd like them to be—you'll be well armed to handle every subsequent step on the path to creating a best-selling consumer product.

NINE QUESTIONS TO SEE IF YOU HAVE A WINNING IDEA

1. What Is My Product?

This sounds easy, but you'd be surprised at how many people have a hard time articulating their idea. If it takes you more than one or two sentences to describe your product or business, you probably don't have a clear enough vision of how it's going to work or whom it's for. Whittling down your concept to its selling essentials will also help you as you find the perfect name for your product. This is the first piece of your branding and marketing efforts, and it will also be the linchpin.

What's in a good brand name? It's catchy, it's descriptive, it's brief, and it's easy to say. You can't get more basic than the name for my first invention, The Earring Organizer. It wasn't flashy, but it left no doubt about what it did or why you'd want one. Don't try to be too clever. Two of my *Shark Tank* entrepreneurs, Marc Newburger and Jeffrey Simon, inventors of a Neoprene wedge that fits between your car seat and the console to keep things like food and phones from slipping where drivers can't reach, considered over eight hundred names, such as the FuGAPaboutit, the Wonder Wedge, the Gap Goalie, and many others. Finally, one day Simon's mother passed through the living room where they were debating names and said, "Guys, it stops stuff from dropping—call it Drop Stop." Bingo.

Once you hit upon the name that says (and sells) it all, make sure to get it trademarked so that no one else can sell a product using that name. In addition, make sure that no one else has already trademarked it, or you could be forced to change your name just as your brand is starting to resonate with consumers. Registering for a trademark is a relatively inexpensive process compared to filing for a patent (see Chapter 6 for extensive details on that) and conducted through the same agency, the U.S. Patent and Trademark Office (USTPO).

2. Does It Solve a Problem?

Many of the greatest inventions were developed because an inventor found a problem so ridiculous, pervasive, or aggravating that he or she felt compelled to do something about it. Earle Dickson invented the Band-Aid because his wife was accident-prone and kept cutting herself in the kitchen. Mary Anderson invented windshield wipers in 1903 when she noticed that streetcar drivers had to lean out of their windows to see during rainstorms. Sarah Breedlove, who reinvented herself as Madam C. J. Walker, invented the hair products that would make her the first African American female millionaire because she was desperate to stop her hair from falling out.

My history of helping my mother find lost pieces of jewelry, missing shoes, or misplaced cosmetics probably explains why so many of my inventions were created to help eradicate clutter and keep people organized. I'm also a busy person, so I am constantly developing or investing in labor- and time-saving devices that will let me do what I have to do quickly so I can get to the activities I actually want to do. I love to eat and I love to cook, but I hate the mess. That inspired a set of no-mess cooking utensils. I jumped on the chance to invest in the Scrub Daddy sponge on *Shark Tank* because, in its one-of-a-kind polymer, I finally found a way to thoroughly clean my glass and ceramic stovetop without scratching it (more about the Scrub Daddy in Chapter 6).

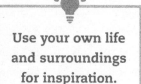

Use your own life and surroundings for inspiration.

I create or invest in solutions to problems I've witnessed or experienced myself. I try to make products that make people's lives easier and better. I won't sell anything that I wouldn't want to use myself. You shouldn't, either. It's easy to spot products that were designed by an inventor or company just out for a buck. You can always tell when making money, and not providing service, value, or quality, was at the forefront of the product designer's mind. People who sincerely want to make their customers' lives better design the best products.

3. Is It Unique?

When you invent something, you can do one of two things: create a whole new product for the market, or improve what's already on the market. I knew my first invention was a hero because I knew nothing like it existed. Most jewelry boxes are all the same—a box with a lid that opens up to reveal little compartments and drawers that hold only one or two pieces neatly. If you own anything more than that, you either have to upgrade to a box the size of a suitcase, or you have to stack your jewelry on top of itself, which inevitably leaves you with a jumbled mess. My earring organizer was compact but it allowed you to see every earring you owned hanging beautifully before you.

With most products I bring to market, whether my own or someone else's, I try to introduce something that the world has never seen. There are many sunglasses on the market, but none that folded down to a tiny two-and-a-half inches like the ones I developed with Neox (and that I wear in the intro to *Shark Tank*). There is plenty of duct tape in the world, but none so strong that it can repair a leaky pipe or a broken shovel like the multipurpose, super tape adhesive called FiberFix. A shoe organizer is just another shoe organizer—until it spins and allows you to store up to 75 articles of clothing, shoes, purses, and belts in a space only inches wide.

If there's one mistake I see entrepreneurs make over and over again, it's to believe so strongly in their invention that they never bother to make sure it's as unique as they think it is. It's good to believe strongly in your invention, but not to the point that you're wearing blinders. About six or seven years ago, I participated in one of Oprah's searches for her Next Big Thing, a contest jointly sponsored by Oprah and QVC to find that year's next great invention. The top three contestants would earn a guest appearance on *Oprah*, and then one would be chosen the winner. Conventions were held across the country in Los Angeles, Philadelphia, and Chicago. Thousands of people showed up to present their ideas to QVC buyers, and I appeared as a consulting expert. People could wait in line to ask me questions for 5 to 10 minutes at a time; and over the course of one day in Los Angeles, I met with almost a thousand participants. It was difficult, because everyone was hopeful, but not everyone had a good idea. But I tried to look for what was good about them and send people on their way with some suggestions about how they could rethink them or make them better.

Then I met a woman who proudly showed me her new baby bag. It was a nicely designed bag with convenient features, particularly in that it could fold out into a changing mat or fold up into a purse. Secretly, though, I didn't think it was that different from so many others already on the market. But I wasn't there to crush anyone's dreams; I was there to advise people and steer them to where they would figure out for themselves if it was a hero or a zero. So that's what I did for this participant. About an hour later, another young woman sat down across from me, carrying her invention—a baby bag. Except for the color, it was exactly the same as the one I'd seen an hour before. Now I had to say something. I told her that I understood how excited she was about it, but I had to share with her the fact that I had seen the same bag just a little while earlier. As I spoke, I prepared myself for her disappointment, maybe even a few fireworks or tears. I got neither. "No way," she said. "It can't be the same as mine." She thanked me for my time, and walked away.

Here's the crazy thing: over the course of the day, I saw five more bags just like that one. Every detail was nearly identical. In total, seven inventors at that one conference had designed the exact same product for the exact same market, and not one of them knew about the others until they met with me and I shared this with them. Amazingly, the six inventors I was able to warn reacted to the news the same way: complete denial. They did not want to believe that all the time, money, and effort they'd put into their invention might have already been for nothing.

You've got to pay attention to what is already for sale and what has been patented or is patent pending (a major reason to hire a patent lawyer—more on that in Chapter 6). It is far more difficult to compete with other products already on the market than to introduce a brand-new, unique product. Of course, it is also a lot harder to come up with a truly unique idea than it is to improve upon something that already exists. So let's say that you're sure you've got a hero of a product, but you also know that you've got competition. What can you do? Where are the areas that can give you an advantage?

Sometimes your price can make you unique. When she was only eleven, Lani Lazzari concocted her first batch of Simple Sugars body scrub to treat her painful, persistent eczema using only natural ingredients. The skin-care market is hugely competitive, and there were already natural scrubs out there claiming to do the same thing as her product. It was for this reason that I chose not to make her an offer when she appeared on *Shark Tank*, even though she was a great contestant. But though using a scrub wasn't a unique solution to the problem of eczema, Simple Sugars was unique in that it provided a hand-made, hand-jarred, hand-labeled natural product for about half the price of its main competitors, while still upholding a high standard of quality. People love it, including Mark Cuban, who did make the deal with Lazzari that allowed her to expand her rapidly growing business.

Sometimes your story can make you unique. Do inventor James Dyson's vacuum cleaners really clean your carpets that much better than the ones you can find at Walmart for much less? He says they do, and he points to a lot of research to back up his claim. For customers who aren't satisfied unless they can eat off the floor, the possibility of "better" makes the higher price point worthwhile. It did for me—I love my Dyson vacuum cleaner. It works and I like seeing the dirt whirl around in the canister. The product looks so cool and the marketing story is so convincing, it is easy to believe that it offers a unique kind of cleaning experience. And that has been worth millions to Dyson.

"Better" does not necessarily trump "unique." If people believe that their problem has been solved, they're probably not going to be interested in a 2.0 version, especially if it costs more than the original. Sometimes people have gotten used to a product being a certain price point, and nothing you do is going to convince them that they should pay more, even if your product is better quality. Or maybe there are people willing to pay, but not enough to propel you out of a niche market. That was why none of the sharks made an offer to Brian Altomare, co-founder of the LugLess baggage shipping service. It is positioned as a less expensive alternative to paying the hefty fees airlines charge to carry luggage beyond your carry-on. But there are already companies that provide this niche service, and none of us sharks could figure out how LugLess could scale and still keep its prices below those of its competitors. It's probably a great service, but despite Altomare's protests at the time of the show, we still saw it as a luxury niche service.

Your 2.0 version might have an advantage if you can create a similar or better quality product for the same price or cheaper.

You can, of course, make a lot of money in a niche market, but it requires a magical combination of great marketing and fortuitous timing. Vending machines used to exclusively carry sodas, so that's what people bought to drink when they were in a hurry or on the go. Bottled water became an alternative, and Evian marketed itself into a status symbol for the healthy set that publicly proclaimed the drinker was healthy, fit, and sophisticated enough to appreciate the difference in taste between natural spring-fed European water and tap water. Then research came out showing how awful soda is for people's health, and bottled water started flying off the shelves. Vending-machine makers adapted so they could carry the popular product. Evian and the like became mainstream products, and a cultural change was born. Today green products, which used to be niche, are picking up speed, especially now that Millennials are growing old enough to make their own purchasing decisions.

Keep this in mind at all times: retailers are always looking for what is new and different. It is in your best interest to try to be that. Not cheaper. Not even just better. Brand-new, different, and surprising—that's what will get the attention of stores, retailers, and shopping networks. Once you've proven you can do business with them, and better yet, once you become an indispensable resource to them and their customers, then you can start moving in on big-brand territory. But in general, it is unwise to try that until you're well established and have the right connections.

4. Is It Something People Will Need or Want?

Most hugely successful inventions are functional and make obligatory tasks easier. Appliances like the clothes dryer and the dishwasher changed homemakers' lives forever. Can you imagine life without zippers, shoelaces, or disposable razors? How about the electric lightbulb? The wheel! At some point, human beings got along without every one of these inventions, but once they became available, they were an indispensable part of daily existence. But you know someone, somewhere, surely looked at that first disposable razor and thought, "Who needs that?" After all, that's what people said about the first cordless phone, and the first computers, too.

Your challenge should be to create something so amazing that once people start to use it, they won't be able to live without it. Create to fulfill people's needs, not their wants, because once they believe they need something your invention is better protected against economic forces. For example, when the economy collapsed in 2008, luxury items stopped selling. Jewelry sales dried up. But people continued to buy disposable razors. If asked which item they wanted more—a beautiful piece of jewelry or a five-pack of disposable razors—most people would probably express desire for the jewelry. But when money gets tight, people don't buy what they want, they buy what they need. Or at least, what they perceive they need.

Small luxuries, like specialty coffees, treats, cosmetics, and haircuts, tend to do well no matter what the state of the economy is, because they're inexpensive ways for people to feel good and look good. They always want to spend money on these basic things. In tough times, these are the ways we treat ourselves and make ourselves feel better.

Any inventor who wants job security should aim to create items that will be perceived as necessities, not luxuries. Accessories are an excellent example. Your phone works just fine and smoothly fits in your pocket without a cool case, but do you know anyone who walks around with an unprotected, undecorated phone? People have been carrying around their reading glasses in their shirt pockets or dangling from chains forever. Each option has some serious drawbacks: in your pocket, your glasses could easily slip out and break, and any chain, even a cool one, is still a granny chain. But no one questioned these options until Rick Hopper invented the ReadeREST, which magnetically and discretely keeps your glasses securely fastened to your shirt or blouse, no matter what. You can still tuck your glasses in your shirt pocket; you can still use a chain. But why on earth would you if you could buy this instead?

5. Is It Demonstrable?

Your customers will have to "get" your product as soon as they see it. Of course, you'll provide investors with fabulous marketing materials, and your customers with excellent copy on the package, but it's not the copy that's going to clinch the sale of your product. Your copy is there only to confirm what has led potential customers to read the copy in the first place: their desire to believe your product works as well as they want it to. Yet we've become a sophisticated buying class, and few people believe everything they read. It's a lot harder, however, for people to dismiss what they see with their own two eyes.

Products that can be easily demonstrated sell really, really well. The late Billy Mays was a genius with demonstrable cleaning products. How could anyone deny the power of OxiClean when you watched him erase grape juice and wine stains from white carpet swatches with just a small spritz of the product, or when you saw one scoop of OxiClean turn the water in a transparent vat of filthy clothes from black to clear? Seeing is definitely believing.

That's how I knew Rick Hopper's ReadeREST was a hero. The other sharks didn't see it that way, though; Robert commented that he thought the product would be the kind of thing sold in gas stations. But they didn't have any experience with the category. I, however, had developed a successful line of reading glasses, and though I didn't wear them myself, I knew that many of my customers, not to mention friends and family members, had the same complaint—they were always losing, misplacing, or breaking their eyewear, whether prescription glasses, sunglasses, or reading glasses. They didn't have a safe, attractive way to keep their glasses on their person when they weren't using them. ReadeREST was the answer. I had already sold hundreds of thousands of reading glasses; it stood to reason that a large portion of those customers would think this was a cool little gadget. They did, and Rick Hopper is now a millionaire with a line of new ideas coming down the pipeline.

6. How Do I Make It?

Will your product be made of plastic or wood, metal or fabric? What type of factory makes your type of product? Where do such factories exist? Is it important to you that you manufacture in the United States, or can your product be made overseas? We'll cover how to select a manufacturer in depth in Chapter 8, but you need to do some preliminary research at this stage in the invention process because the answers will immediately give you a ballpark figure of how much it will cost you to make your product, which will then tell you how much you can charge for it. And price matters a great deal. If your target market can't afford your product, you're in trouble. In addition, the majority of consumers in our post-recession society will continue to feel a pinch for years as they come to grips with the fact that the price of necessities like food and fuel have risen but paychecks have not. We'll discuss pricing in Chapter 4.

Another question to which the answers will inform pricing, manufacturing, and even selling is: how big will your product be? The bigger your product, the harder it will be to sell, not only because of pricing concerns but also because retailers have only so much square footage for display and storage, whether for stock in the back or in their warehouse. It would be a shame to meet a retailer who loves your product but can't sell it because they don't have the room. Obviously, the size of a product won't matter if its size is part of what makes it wonderful. Refrigerators were once almost half the size they are now, until people started demanding more space, not just for food storage but also for home square footage as well.

7. Who Is Your Target Market?

Whenever possible, invent for the masses. There is a niche market for products, but it's easier to design something that is useful, with broad appeal, at a price point that the majority of people can afford. The broader your audience, the better your chances of making large numbers of sales. There are many examples of products made for specific segments of society that have sold spectacularly well, of course. The kids' market is filled with them. Who knows, maybe you've got the next Beanie Baby or Silly Bandz on your hands. Who could have predicted the Slinky would still be selling after sixty years? Luck could be on your side. But it's better if you don't count on it. If you insist that you have knowledge about a certain demographic that makes you confident you can sell to that specific group, make plans to branch out as soon as possible once you've made your mark on that audience.

8. Is It Safe?

It is not acceptable to leave it to the marketplace to decide whether a product poses a serious risk or not. If you suspect your product could be dangerous even when used by its intended audience for its intended purpose, it is imperative that you refrain from taking it to market until you have eliminated the risk. Toys, in particular, need to be vetted extremely carefully. Kids put objects in their mouths—even children who should be old enough to know better. You don't want to be the next BuckyBalls, those rare-earth magnets that were not just recalled but banned because children kept swallowing them. But it's not just inventors of children's toys and products who need to be careful. Food is extremely risky, as are energy beverages and baby formulas. Anything that requires batteries is going to have to go through its own battery of tests. Count on just about anything you create being tested for lead content.

9. Is It a Consumable?

There are a few product categories: apparel, cosmetics, soft goods (like textiles or fabrics), food, and consumables. Consumable goods are fabulous products because they provide you with continual revenue; they must be replaced once they're depleted. They can be the household items that appear frequently on your shopping list, like razors, dryer sheets, vitamins, and soap. They're in your office, too—paper, pens, and toner are all consumable. I wish I invented consumables! Somehow, I'm always struck with ideas for durable goods instead. Though I don't make consumables, I love to invest in them, and most investors feel the same way. Think about that when you're developing your idea.

LET'S SAY YOU'VE ANSWERED ALL nine hero-or-zero questions. What do your answers mean?

It depends. If you've decided that your idea isn't as robust as you thought it was, that means a lot, because the earlier you determine that you're running with the wrong idea, the sooner you can start thinking up the right one. But aside from that, even if you answered yes to all of the questions above, nothing will confirm without a doubt that your invention is a hero except putting it out on the market and watching people buy it. If no one does, you have your answer. Still, you can improve your chances of success by doing market research. A drawing will not be enough; people will need to be able to see your product, touch it, and use it. If your answer to the questions in this chapter gave you reason to believe that your idea has commercial potential, you're ready to take the next leap. It's time to build a prototype.

HERO OR ZERO CHECKLIST

Some indicators that your product may be a hero:

❑ It serves a function.

❑ It solves a problem.

❑ It is unique.

❑ People want or need it.

❑ It is demonstrable.

❑ You can sell it at a reasonable price for what it is.

❑ It is appealing to the mass market.

❑ There are not a lot of competitors.

❑ It is a consumable.

❑ It poses no obvious danger to the public.

❑ You can explain it in a few short sentences.

❑ You have a patent or patents.

❑ It appeals to a wide age range.

❑ It's manageable in size.

If you can check off eight or more of these, your product might be a hero.

3

YOU'VE GOT A GREAT IDEA, NOW WHAT?

"If you are interested, you'll do what's convenient. If you are committed, you'll do what it takes."

—JOHN ASSARAF

ON HIS FIRST DAY OF WORK AS A MAILROOM CLERK AT THE MEGA-corporation Hudsucker Industries, Norville Barnes, the hero of Joel and Ethan Coen's screwball comedy *The Hudsucker Proxy*, shows his coworker a simple drawing of a circle on a rumpled piece of paper. "This is my ticket upstairs," he says proudly. "You know, for kids!" The coworker looks at him in dumbfounded confusion. A few minutes later, Barnes takes advantage of a moment in front of Sidney Mussberger, the company's chairman, to pull the drawing out of his shoe. Carefully making sure the circle is shown right side up, he says, "You know, for kids!" Mussberger glares at him like he's a moron. Later, Barnes makes a prototype, but as he energetically makes his pitch for what we now know is a hula hoop, the company board stares at him uncomprehendingly. Even after Barnes's invention is produced, in spite of the large color poster of a child spinning a hula hoop around his waist and front-row placement in the window of the town toy store, no one buys it. It isn't until the store owner throws the plastic rings out into the street and a little boy picks it up and starts to twirl it around his waist, to the delight and astonishment of his friends, that the toy becomes a hit.

The movie is a satirical take on corporate America, but with these scenes it humorously depicts the truth of what one *Shark Tank* entrepreneur said when she came into the tank to pitch: a product can sound like a really great idea, but it's not until people can see it, feel it, or touch it that they can experience the wow factor that leads to sales. Poor Norville Barnes didn't even have the benefit of a great-sounding idea, and on paper his design was meaningless. But once the product made it into the hands of its intended audience, his invention finally revealed its true bestselling potential.

It's just a movie, but in its exaggerated way *The Hudsucker Proxy* illustrates why a well-designed prototype, tested by the people you think will most want to use it, is crucial to the success of your product. Every step you take from this point, from conducting market research, to getting funding, to landing your first sale, will depend entirely upon the perfection of your working prototype. Your prototype is what can transform a potential consumer or retail buyer's reaction to your idea from a tepid, "How nice," to an insistent, "How fast can we get these in the store?" Plus, this is your chance to make your product the best version of itself it can possibly be. Try not to be too easily satisfied. Until your prototype is exactly right, it's not ready to share with anyone. Introducing your product to the world is no different from introducing yourself for a job interview: you've got about ten seconds to make a good first impression, and you only get one chance. So make it count!

Another reason why prototypes are important is that the trial-and-error process of making one teaches you everything you need to know about your product: what materials are best suited to make it, how complicated the manufacturing process will be, how easy it will be for a customer to assemble it, and whether it even really works. It allows you to fix problems now while it's cheap, not later on, when you've got 20,000 units suffering from a design flaw.

Today my factories and suppliers make my prototypes. We've worked together for a long time, so they know me well and have a sense of what I want. I can grab a napkin or piece of paper and sketch out the approximate dimensions of my idea, and their design engineers can draft more sophisticated drawings from that. They send me a first sample, and then we perfect the design along the way. I send them fabric swatches or color ideas, often using Pantone Matching System (PMS) color books (a system that allows you to explain and share the colors you want for anything from packaging to fabrics to book covers; say "PMS 326," and every designer knows what you mean). We email ideas back and forth. Once I'm satisfied, the design is sent to one of my manufacturers, who uses the drawing and other information to create a perfect sample of my product. So I have a lot of help with my prototypes. But back when I was just starting out, all I had were my own two hands and a set of power tools that I didn't know how to use.

THE FIRST DRAFT

Many people find inspiration in the shower or other environments where they get a chance to relax and shut out the noise and distractions of the outside world. I often have eureka moments when I'm sitting in an airplane, where there are no phones ringing and no interruptions. It's one of the only places I get some quiet time to think. However, the first bolt of inspirational lightning that launched my career hit me during a massage. My friend Pam was a massage therapist, and one day while she was working on me, we started commiserating about one of our pet peeves: the annoying fact that there was no good way to store your earrings. You wound up having to throw them all in a heap in your jewelry box if you owned more than a few pair. You'd lose a back or find only one of the two just when you were in a hurry to get out of the house. My head still squashed into the massage table's face hole, I sighed, "There has to be a better way."

And that's when, literally in a flash, like a lightning bolt, a picture appeared in my mind, instantly and fully formed. Sliding earring stands, one behind another, on top of a base. They'd slide to the left and to the right, so you could see everything at a quick glance. It would hold pierced and clip-on earrings and take up a small space. It was different from anything else out there. Like all entrepreneurs, I was certain it was hero and that every woman on earth would want one.

> **All entrepreneurs think everybody will need and want their products.**

This was not the first time I'd had an idea that I thought could be a commercial hit. Not long before that eureka moment, I'd had an idea for a collection of modern, updated fairy tales, which I called *Fairy Tales for the Nineties*. They were alternatives to the traditional versions that were so sexist and unnecessarily scary. They needed to be updated for our times. I had written several stories when, one day, while checking out purchases at a Barnes & Noble, I happened to look down and see an easel holding a copy of a book called *Politically Correct Bedtime Stories*.

The book's jacket was prominently displayed, and on it there was a starburst saying, *"New York Times* Bestseller!" Well, that was that. Of course, there was no guarantee that my book would have made it big, but if there already was a book of modernized fairy tales on the bestseller list, the idea was on the right track, and I had just missed the boat. The next time I had an idea I thought was a hero, I was going to act on it immediately (and think more about question no. 3 in the previous chapter!).

After my idea hit me on the massage table, I raced home with my mind on fire. It was July. If I wanted to get my product into stores for Christmas, I was going to have to get moving fast (little did I know that most buyers shore up their fourth-quarter orders, which include the holiday season, in April!).

When Dan walked through the door, I said, "Honey, I have a great idea!" He thought the organizer sounded interesting and told me to sketch it out. I pulled out a sheet of paper, a pencil, and a ruler, and started drawing. Once I had transposed the picture in my head onto the page, I started to think about the dimensions it would need to be. I thought about my space, and my mother's, and the bathrooms, bedrooms, and closets of all the women I knew. I wanted to create an organizer that would hold three times as many earrings as the typical jewelry box, yet be compact enough that it wouldn't sit like the Hulk on a woman's vanity or bathroom counter.

My drawing skills are just okay. I tried to be as meticulous and neat as I could be, but my style is kind of sloppy, big, and wild— true to my artistic nature. When I draw on a pad of paper, my columns aren't straight; I write on a diagonal. Dan, on the other hand, writes in neat, precise little lines. He is detail-oriented like an engineer. So once I got the basic design of the organizer down, I asked him to redraw it. He pulled out some graph paper and drew the organizer according to my specifications. We talked and drew and erased and measured and drew some more until finally Dan handed me a perfect representation of the organizer I had envisioned in my head. It was beautiful. It held one hundred pairs of pierced or clip-on earrings on five sliding stands that allowed you to see all of the earrings at a quick glance.

Looking back, it's incredible that Dan didn't question whether this idea was really something I should pursue. He's cautious—not at all the type to push the envelope. And yet, in this instance he was on board from the minute I told him about my idea.

If you're artistically challenged, or your idea is complicated and you're unable to make your own accurate design, and you don't have someone like Dan to help you, you can hire a design engineer to draw it for you. Design engineers will work with you to draft a computer-aided design (CAD), which is essentially a 3-D blueprint that can be viewed and spun around on your pc, then manipulated, tested, and altered before being sent to a prototype maker or manufacturer. In an increasingly common process called CAD/CAM (computer-aided design/computer-aided manufacturing), the prototype maker's or manufacturer's computers send the CAD data to the machines to direct them how to make the product.

Commissioning a CAD can be a pricey option, though. If money is an issue, you might consider going to a local college or university and hiring an engineering student to design your CAD. One advantage to the CAD is that you can sit with designers while they're working and see your virtual product take shape on the computer monitor. This gives you the ability to tweak things along the way before actually trying to build it. CADs are impressive in their quality and accuracy; the finished drawing makes it look like your product is going to jump off the page.

CREATING A MOCK-UP

Many times I've picked up a new product on the market and wondered if the person who designed it ever actually tried to use it. You can always tell the items that an individual or a company designed just to make a buck. A pancake batter dispenser that leaves all the blueberries crushed and smeared against the inside of the dispenser instead of leaving them plump and whole in the pancake on the griddle—that couldn't have been designed by someone who loves blueberry pancakes, or who had even tested it (testing and retesting your product is really important). A lipstick holder too shallow to properly hold a lipstick couldn't have been designed by a person who actually wears lipstick and who wanted to create a better way to store her makeup. You tend to know what a market needs if *you* are the market. Of course, you can successfully create products for demographics beyond your own; you'll just need to be extra careful with your market research and how you target that audience.

Stories abound of inventors using everyday materials from home, like cardboard, clay, foam, wood, and disassembled household products, to create precursors to prototypes—called mock-ups—that test their designs and ensure they actually work. Rick Hopper created models of his magnetized glasses holder by bending paper clips into various shapes and experimenting with different-strength magnets. The creators of the Drop Stop experimented with multiple types of stuffing and stitching before deciding upon the final design of their invention. I wanted to be sure my design would work the way I thought it would before committing to the expense of a prototype. How hard could it be? All

I needed to do was cut a few
round rods and crossbars to
size, drill a few holes, and my
organizer would be complete.
I even knew where I could
get my hands on the right
tools—a basement woodshop
in rural Illinois that belonged
to my husband's grandfather.
The problem was, being a

Do everything yourself,
except when you
absolutely can't. Know
when to ask for help
or let the experts do
their job.

city girl, though I had access to tools, I had no idea how to use
them. I needed help. So I turned to my husband, Dan, who was
extremely handy and had plenty of experience.

I've gone on record saying that, in principle, inventors should
do as much as possible themselves because it is cheaper than hiring everything out and, more important, the experience and expertise you gain sets you up much better for success later. With
enough time, you can learn how to do anything. The problem is,
of course, that some jobs are just out of our league; and when
time is short, speed and efficiency sometimes need to take pre-
cedence over principle. In addition, if you're going for the mass
market, you're eventually going to have to navigate certain rules
regarding your industry. You'll have to adhere to previously unknown safety regulations, and you have to learn about labeling
for the American market, the European market, or whatever market you're planning to sell to. Each has its own rules and regulations; they are not always one and the same. It's unlikely you
have the training to deal with that on your own. Even if you were
capable of making your product on your own in large enough
quantities to fulfill mass orders, you wouldn't want to be forced
to stop selling because you didn't research and comply with the
laws governing the manufacture or use of your product.

Whenever you do ask someone to take over a job, make sure to stay close to the process and learn as much as possible. Shadow the person you hire, if you can. Talk with the individual, watch, and listen so that by the time the person is done, you are on your way to becoming an expert in this area, too. As long as you take the opportunity to educate yourself, any money you spend on hiring experts to help or advise you will be well spent.

Dan and I drove to his grandfather's woodshop together. I hovered nearby as he cut the wood according to my specifications. He was patient, taking my nerves in stride. Parts cut, we assembled the organizer, and then I spent a long time attaching earrings to the rods and moving all the parts around to make sure that each piece worked the way I thought it should. Much to Dan's chagrin, it didn't work exactly right. The panels didn't slide smoothly and there wasn't enough room for all the different types of earrings a woman might have in her collection. So we started over from scratch. Hours later, at the end of the day, I finally had a crude but functional earring organizer that worked exactly the way I had envisioned.

It worked, but it wasn't pretty. What materials was I going to use? I wasn't an artisan craftsman handcrafting jewelry organizers to a select few; I wanted to make my product available to every woman who loved jewelry. So wood was out. Besides, all along I'd imagined that the organizer would be clear and sparkly. I've always loved the way light reflects off of crystal; if I could facet the sides, it might mimic that effect. And a clear material would match any setting, which was important because no woman was going to use an organizer that clashed with her décor. Glass would be too fragile and expensive, so obviously I was going to need to use plastic. But plastic might look cheap, and I wanted to create something beautiful. I kept thinking. What material is clear or neutral, durable, and relatively inexpensive? In the end, it was my prototype maker who came up with the answer. He used Lucite to create my prototype, but he suggested that in the future, polystyrene would be the right material for the final product because it was a less expensive plastic, yet still water clear.

MAKING A PROTOTYPE

How do you find a prototype maker? Today, all you have to do is Google the word "prototype" and your city or state, and the Internet will offer you a list of prototype makers in your area. But this was 1996, so I pulled out the Yellow Pages and looked up "prototype makers." Sure enough, there was more than one located in Chicago. But how was I supposed to choose?

As I would learn, all prototype makers are not alike. Each one specializes in fabricating products from a certain material. Some make products out of plastic, others out of metal, some out of wood, and others work with fabric and textiles, to name a few, so the first thing you need to find out is who makes prototypes out of the materials you need. Then pay a visit and interview the prototype maker. Ask to see models they have made, find out what they charge, and assess whether they are a good fit for you. Once you're satisfied with the cost and quality of their product, and your

Any reputable prototype maker, manufacturer, or other company specializing in helping entrepreneurs and inventors bring new products to market should be willing to sign a nondisclosure agreement that forbids them to discuss, share, or otherwise use any part of your idea or design. If they refuse, walk away.

prototype maker has signed a nondisclosure agreement—very important if you have not already filed for a patent—you will hand over the design of your invention and they will refer to your specifications to create a functional model that you can use when conducting market research and giving pitches.

Earlier I mentioned that more and more inventors are working with CAD designers to create detailed and realistic designs of their product. Increasingly, your prototype maker will use a 3-D printer to create your model. Rather than cut shapes out of materials and then assemble the parts the way traditional machines would, 3-D printers build up the product by putting down layers of materials—liquefied plastic, powdered metals, softened ceramic, or nylon, for example—which is why another term for the process of building objects with 3-D printing is "additive manufacturing." Just a few years ago, 3-D printing, used in rapid prototyping (RP), still seemed the realm of sci-fi, but it is rapidly going mainstream. One day, we may all be printing products on demand—including your invention, perhaps—with the same ease and convenience as we print our documents at home. For now, though, CAD design and 3-D printing are still highly specialized processes, which require a lot of skill and training. A simple Google search will reveal that there are 3-D printers catering to small business owners and entrepreneurs located all across the country.

My prototype wasn't cheap. There are many types of proto-

Even today $10,000 is considered a high price for a prototype. It's unlikely yours will cost you anywhere near that much. The costs will vary widely, depending on your product's size, shape, and the materials from which it is made.

types, each one representing various levels of sophistication and detail, but the kind I needed, and the one any new inventor intent on selling his or her idea will need, is called a "pre-production prototype." It is essentially identical to the finished product, but is made using a one-off mold, which is a lot cheaper to pay for than a permanent mold. It cost me $10,000 to make.

Yet I was willing to spend the money, for I was sure that the more professionally made and beautiful my prototype, the easier it would be for people to fall in love with it and I would get the sales.

Get your ducks in a row as soon as possible, so that when your orders start to come in, you're ready to go. There are many other things you can get started on while waiting for your prototype to be made: contact retailers, look for manufacturing options, investigate your funding options, set your price, file for your patent and trademark. With the exception of the final two, nothing on this list will cost you anything but time, so you risk nothing.

I hoped my prototype would be my ticket to those holiday sales I wanted. I could pre-sell with it. I could take it with me to stores to show to buyers. Whether they were the consumers I knew I'd have to poll for market research, or retail buyers selecting products for their customers, I wanted to make it as easy as possible for people to imagine the organizer on a woman's dressing table. It would help me make sure people were willing to buy my invention and save me from making the worst mistake of my life. I had an incredibly strong gut instinct that I had a hero on my hands, but I wanted to make sure my instincts were correct. Unsubstantiated enthusiasm would surely lead me to make a mistake, so I needed to do unbiased market research first.

My prototype maker's suggestion that I make my invention out of polystyrene, and his additional advice that I might need something called an injection molder, sent me on my next research binge. I didn't know the first thing about plastics, so I went back to the Yellow Pages and looked under "plastics." And there was a list of companies that manufactured plastic in Chicago. This was a relief, because I'd already made up my mind that I was going to do what I could to work with local companies so that at all times I could keep a close eye on the production, packaging, and any other processes necessary to usher my product onto retail shelves. But aside from "plastics," there were other words staring up at me from those business directory pages. Thermoforming. Extrusion. It turned out there were different types of plastic manufacturing processes, and I was going to have to figure out which one I needed. It seemed as if every time I got one question answered, ten more popped up. Methodically, I started researching, reading, and making calls to educate myself about what I would need to do to bring my product to life. And sure enough, my prototype maker was right: I needed an injection molder, a factory that mass-produces products by using large machines to inject liquefied plastic into molds.

> **Ignorance is never a good excuse for stalling. You can get any information you need if you're willing to do the research.**

You have all the information at your fingertips that you need to get your invention made. If, then, I could figure out how to get my prototype made when my only resources were the business pages and whatever books I could lug home from the library, today you can use the Internet to find a reliable prototype maker, as well as manufacturer, packager, sales rep, or any other resource you need. It is worth the time and effort to educate yourself as thoroughly as possible about every aspect of your business, from design to manufacturing to packaging. Absorbing all that knowledge will be instrumental in protecting yourself from being taken advantage of and for negotiating the best deals possible.

MAKE OPPORTUNITY WORK FOR YOU

Before devoting myself full time to my organizer, I had worked with a woman named Georgia, and a day or so after finding out that there was polystyrene and injection molding somewhere in my future, Dan and I attended her son's wedding. We didn't know anyone there, but we looked forward to a fun evening. I was midway through my appetizer and deep in conversation with the neighbor to my right when I felt Dan firmly tap me on the hand. I turned to him to see him grinning broadly. Leaning in, he said, "You're not going to believe this."

"What?" I replied.

"Guess what every person at this table does?"

"What?"

"They're all plastic injection molders." He grinned with a Cheshire Cat smile. "That guy over there," he pointed across the table, "is a toolmaker. And these other guys here? Also injection molders. But guess what? Georgia's husband owns an injection molding factory about twenty minutes away from us." Unbelievable! What we needed had just fallen into our laps.

I love that anecdote because I've always believed in karma and destiny. I needed an injection molder, and there I was at a wedding where everyone at my table was in the plastic injection mold business. Georgia and I had talked often, but her husband's profession had simply never come up, so I had no idea what he did for a living! It was a brilliant stroke of luck, and I was grateful for it. But even if I had never gone to that wedding, I would have eventually found every person sitting at that table. I would have hunted them down and introduced myself and explained why they were going to want to do business with me. Success takes doggedness!

A few days after the wedding, I visited the tool-making shop with my drawings and prototype in hand (we'll cover what to look for in a manufacturer in Chapter 8). I wanted to get a general idea of what it would cost to make the earring organizer so that I could start to think about pricing. The owner took me on a tour of his shop, helped me understand how everything worked, explained to me what tools I would need to make my product, and gave me a quote. Then I went to the injection-molding factory and had the same tour and conversation there. I found out that it would cost me $120,000 to make the three molds necessary to manufacture my earring organizer in the United States.

Ten thousand dollars had been a hefty sum to pay for my prototype. But $120,000 was eye-popping. And that was just for the tools. I knew I was still going to have to pay for graphic design, packaging, inventory, and other expenses; I was going to have to take out a bank loan to get this done. But I wasn't daunted. I did what my dad always taught me to do—I thought, "What's the worst thing that could happen?" Answer: It won't work out. But I had a plan in place, and I was determined to make it work, so I forged ahead.

Now, in the short amount of time it took my prototype to be made, I had created a questionnaire. And as soon as the prototype was ready, I had taken it and the questionnaire to the streets of Chicago to conduct some thorough market research. The results confirmed what my innate instinct was screaming at me, which was that I had hit upon an idea whose time had come.

PROTOTYPE TO-DO LIST:

❏ Finalize the dimensions of your product.

❏ Research the materials you will need to create it. Talk to industry professionals to get recommendations.

❏ Contact at least two designers so you can compare bids for a CAD design.

❏ Get the names and locations of at least two prototype makers so you can compare bids.

❏ Confirm that your prototype maker will sign a nondisclosure agreement.

❏ Learn from the advice these professionals give you along the way.

4

RESEARCH YOUR MARKET

"Forget mistakes. Forget failure. Forget everything except what you're going to do now and do it. Today is your lucky day."

—WILL DURANT

IT'S SO EASY FOR INVENTORS TO GET CARRIED AWAY IN THEIR enthusiasm. With every new idea, we are convinced we've created an amazing solution to a big problem, or that there is a hole in the market that only our invention can fill. But sometimes, if we're not careful, we can misjudge the market. Sometimes the problems that make us want to tear out our hair are simply mild annoyances to others. Sometimes our solution is more problematic than the problem it's trying to solve. All entrepreneurs are passionate about their product. However, there's passion, and there's delusion. Market research can confirm that your invention warrants the first, and it can save you from the latter. It's the reality check on your unbridled enthusiasm and ambition.

Market research can also help you avoid making one of the most common mistakes of new inventors, which is to manufacture a product even before getting a single order. This is a terrible idea. Inventors who fall into this trap usually think they are being models of preparedness. They think that they are going to get hit with a tsunami of orders, and they're taking proper precautions to make sure they can fulfill them. But ordering product before receiving orders isn't an example of preparedness; it's one of the biggest mistakes entrepreneurs make. First, you've put yourself on the hook to pay for all those units, even though you have no guarantee of revenue. Second, you now have the additional burden of paying for storage. Third, when you order your inventory too soon, you're wasting the money you paid for your prototype because you're undermining one of the main reasons you got it in the first place—to conduct your market research. Placing an order too soon with a manufacturer has ruined countless inventors. Avoid adding yourself to this unfortunate list, and conduct your market research rigorously. Done properly, it will add substance to your pitch and to your claim that millions of customers are just waiting to get their hands on your invention.

Your market research will focus on three primary areas of interest:

- First, you will want to know as much about the competition as possible. Are there other products out there like your invention, and if so, who makes them, who buys them, and how well do they sell?
- Second, you will want to be informed about the consumer market in general. What is the state of the economy, and how is it affecting consumers' spending habits? What's on trend right now?
- Finally, you want to know specifically whether people will like your invention and recognize its usefulness and appeal.

For the first two types of investigations, you're researching information that has already been documented, and it's the kind of data you can get by scouring the Internet, the news, and well-researched blogs, and by reading trade reports, white papers, and any other previously conducted market research you can find.

To get real insight into that third area of interest, which taps into your potential customers' wants and needs, you need to go straight to the customers themselves.

THREE KEYS TO GETTING USEFUL FEEDBACK

When you're doing your market research, keep this in mind: you're not looking for positive feedback; you're looking for *accurate* feedback. It will do you absolutely no good to get over-

The only useful feedback is accurate feedback.

whelming positive response to your invention if you've asked the wrong people the wrong questions in the wrong way. In fact, inadvertently soliciting inaccurate feedback could be equally ruinous as placing an order with a manufacturer before you have any orders. So don't do it.

Let's discuss the three keys to obtaining accurate feedback through market research.

1. Anonymity

Family members and friends are often an important source of emotional support for new inventors. However, when you are conducting your market research, you should avoid them entirely. Do not ask the opinion of people who love you, like you, or even know you, because they will either (a) refuse to hurt your feelings and tell you they like your idea, no matter what they really think; or (b) harbor jealous feelings and tell you they don't like it, no matter what they really think. You never know. People are either for you or against you; they're never neutral.

2. The Right Questions

Leave no stone unturned. Create a written questionnaire that asks as many detailed questions as possible, but not so many it overwhelms your respondent. If people have been gracious enough to stop to give you a few minutes of their time, don't make them regret their decision by handing them a packet the thickness of a dictionary. A quick one-pager will be sufficient, listing maybe eight or ten key questions. You don't want to take up too much of people's time. Believe me, that would certainly affect the kind of answers they offered, assuming they even completed your survey.

As most people know, the way in which you ask a question can influence the reply you get and will skew your results. For example, consider the different answers you'd get to these questions:

1. Unrecycled paper comprises about 40 percent of the amount of solid waste in our landfills. What do you think of this desk-top automatic paper dissolver?

2. Would you use this desk-top paper dissolver?

Your questions should be short and neutral:

- Do you like this product?
- If you don't like it, why?
- Would you buy it?
- Do you have a need for it?
- Where would you expect to find this?

- Would you buy this for someone else? If yes, who?
- Would you buy multiples? If yes, why?
- What would you pay for it?

For that last question, you would include multiple-choice an-swers. For example, if you wanted to sell the product for under $25, you'd ask the most important question: What would you pay for this? You could offer your respondents the options of $14.99, $19.99, $29.99, and $34.99. By going from the extreme low to the extreme high, you're not steering people toward a tiny range, which allows you to get a good grasp of how people value your product.

3. A Large Cross Section of People

You always want to seek out the opinions of your target audi-ence, of course, but don't put limits on yourself or your inven-tion. You never know; you may think that your market is women between the ages of 30 and 50, and then discover that in fact it's women between the ages of 20 and 30, as well as men. My mar-ket research informed me that one of my major assumptions was flat-out wrong. I thought every woman would want one of my organizers, because I thought every woman liked jewelry and had a collection of it. It never occurred to me that there were women who didn't care for jewelry and owned little, if any. That was a good thing to know. Keep your reach broad. And if you find that your market skews in a direction you hadn't anticipated, go with it. Follow the consumers' lead, but go with your overall response. Perhaps 20 percent of the women I spoke with said they didn't own a lot of jewelry, but the majority did.

WHERE TO DO YOUR RESEARCH

Social Media

Not very long ago, unless you were a large business with the funds to pay a market research company to do the work for you, the only way to find out more about the potential market for your invention would be to question your circle of friends and acquaintances (which, as we just discussed, is not informative), or to canvass the population where you live. It just wasn't feasible for a first-time inventor to test a broader national or even global market. All that changed with the Internet and social media.

Almost every social media outlet has search capabilities that allow you to target potential buyers and listen to the conversations they are having about the problem your invention could solve. If you choose, you can sometimes even engage in dialogue with your market, asking questions to elicit responses that will help you confirm your beliefs about your invention and the market you hope to serve. I often ask my Facebook fans to weigh in on products I'm developing. On Twitter, you can do hashtag searches or follow trends, and get direct, uninhibited, and honest insight into how your potential consumers think and feel about any number of topics, brands, and products—straight from the horses' mouths.

You can customize those searches to give you results for a specific geographic location, or you can click on "Global" to get worldwide results. If you wanted to get really specific, you could use Twitter's advanced search option, which could conceivably help you find out how many people sent tweets containing, for example, the words "luggage" or "Christmas trees" from a location near, say, Salem, Oregon. You can conduct less intense research on Pinterest, which is a mecca for anyone passionate about food, clothing, accessories, crafts, or home décor, among many other visually appealing categories, by searching any of the pin categories or doing a word search. Typing in "wine aerator" shows you an endless scroll of beautiful images of different wine aerator designs. Which ones have been repinned the most? What are the names of the boards on which they've been repinned? If you see images of something that relates to your product, is it on boards with titles like, "Things I Can't Live Without" or "My Favorites"? That should tell you something. On Facebook, you can take advantage of Graph Search and look at who has publicly proclaimed interest in an area relevant to your product. For example, if you asked to see "People who like martial arts," you'd be privy to a list of over a million people. In addition, you could see the geographic area where they live, and often what they read, what shows they watch, and what brands they like. From that you might be able to extrapolate spending habits and consumer preferences.

Many times you can use these social media search options to gather information about how your audience feels about your competitors, and what your competitor is doing to serve them. From some you can get a general idea of how often your customers shop, how much money they spend, and where and when they spend it. And most of the time you can get this information for free. If you've got some money to spend, you can pay to get access to even greater amounts of detail on the people who might buy your product.

Online Survey Companies

These are terrific and inexpensive tools for expanding the scope of the population you'd like to question regarding your product and your market. One of the most popular is SurveyMonkey. There you can send questionnaires to as many members of their "Audience"—regular survey takers who have been recruited to answer additional surveys like yours—as you like. The cost of conducting the survey is based on your targeting criteria, the size of your audience, and the number of completed surveys. You can tailor questions to find out about your target customers' reading, buying, and entertainment consumption habits, but you can also be a little more nuanced and find out, for example, what factors influence them most at the point of purchase, or what considerations they make before spending money.

Crowdfunding Campaigns

Some people gain valuable information by doing a mock auction of their item via crowdfunding. These are entrepreneurs willing to take the risk of revealing their products online without the protection of a patent. You'll see people on fund-raising sites posting photographs of their products while trying to raise money. It works; when people get a glimpse of something cool, they often jump at the chance to be a part of its creation, especially if one of the rewards for donating is the product itself.

These inventors are gambling that once they've obtained their funding, they can get their product into retailers and build brand recognition and loyalty before any competitor has time to copy them and eat at their market share. But revealing your product online before you have a patent is something to consider carefully. I personally recommend trying to have some coverage—it's always safer if you have a patent or one pending. Yet it's a double-edged sword. On the one hand, revealing the product will allow you to raise dollars to help you get started, and you may even get contacted by a manufacturer, a manufacturer's rep, or a distributor. They often watch sites like Kickstarter and Indiegogo to find products that might be right for them (we'll talk more about fund-raising sites like these in Chapter 5). On the other hand, once you put your product online, you are extremely vulnerable to poachers.

Some overseas manufacturers or nefarious types will watch these sites to get ideas for products and then do them without you. Factories surf the Internet all the time looking at popular products, even bestselling items on websites like QVC or Amazon, to find new ideas and products they can knock off. I can't stomach the idea of seeing someone else steal the product that you've put so much work into and that you were hoping would provide a better future for yourself and your loved ones. However, it's an extremely personal choice, and not every product is patentable. Also, for some inventors the cost of applying for a patent is prohibitive, and everyone's tolerance for risk differs.

> Despite the risks inherent in exposing your product too soon, Kickstarter, one of the most widely used fund-raising sites, has become a de facto market research resource. If you post your product and your story, and it gains popularity and the donations come pouring in, that's a good sign that you're on to something.

For some, the opportunity to get funding or gain brand awareness might outweigh the risk of losing control over their ideas. Make the best, most financially sound choice you can, but be aware of how very hard it is to protect a product once its image gets passed around online. Once it's out there, the world can see it, for better or for worse.

Face-to-Face Market Research

Social media provide entrepreneurs with an effective, inexpensive, and sometimes absolutely free way to talk to your target audience and find out how they feel about the problem you're trying to solve with your invention. Yet in these days when SurveyMonkey and Twitter can give you access to almost any consumer market from Miami to Anchorage, the best way to gauge how people are going to react to your product, and predict whether they will buy it, is still with a hands-on introduction.

An inventor doing market research for a new product is a bit like a new parent introducing his or her baby to the world. However, only a monster would peer at a new parent's infant and say, "Wow, that is one ugly baby." New inventors out in the field have no protection against such blunt assessments, however. You need to be okay with that before heading out. In fact, you need to insist on brutal honesty, regardless of how much it hurts, because doing so will save you from potentially much greater pain later.

Make sure the people you talk to understand that they will be doing you a disservice if they sugarcoat their feedback. In fact, when I did market research for my first invention, I found that one of the best ways to ensure objective replies, and avoid making people feel put on the spot or obligated to be nice, was to avoid telling them that the product I was asking them to evaluate was mine. I'd just tell them I was conducting market research on a new product, and no one ever thought to ask me who had designed it. Only if someone was really going crazy over it would I admit it was mine, because I thought they might be willing to spend a little more time with me so I could continue to delve even deeper with questions.

You might think that it could be nerve-wracking and uncomfortable to ask perfect strangers to pass judgment on something that means so much to you. Maybe it is for some, but it wasn't for me. I like honesty. I can deal with it, and I feel it helps me to make good, smart decisions. Most entrepreneurs I know felt the same way when they did their market research. I couldn't wait to get out there and find out what consumers had to say, because my financial success or ruin depended on it.

If you do feel awkward, never let people know it. Think about it this way: you've got an advantage over telephone pollsters in that you can show a friendly face, make a little joke, and use props. Do not be shy, yet do not be pushy. Don't start out with the sales gimmick of asking some kind of goofy question to which most people can say yes. Be extremely careful not to get too close and invade people's physical space so that you make them feel uncomfortable. Simply approach people in a friendly and un-threatening manner, and in your nicest, most polite tone, say, "Would you mind giving me your opinion about a brand-new product?" If they're not in a hurry to get anywhere, and you don't make them feel pressured or uncomfortable, a surprising number of people will stop and hear you out.

Use levity always. No one minds spending time with a person who makes them laugh. You might offer them a small trinket like a pen or a flashlight in appreciation for their time. Everybody loves freebies, no matter how small, and, hey, if you're trying to build a brand, handing out inexpensive promotional gifts is a good way to start getting name recognition.

You can conduct face-to-face market research anywhere, such as at carnivals, flea markets, festivals, shopping malls, and parks. You'd be amazed at how productive a few days at a street fair can be. Anyplace where a large cross section of the popula-tion congregates, and that doesn't charge you an arm and a leg to set up a booth or table to exhibit your prototype, is where you want to be. Be creative, and be brave. Some of the most pro-lific and successful inventors got their start demonstrating their products out of the backs of their cars, on the side of the road, in parking lots, and on street corners.

I know that pounding the pavement works, because that's

what I did. When I designed my first invention, I felt in my gut that I had created a unique solution to a near-universal problem for women who wore earrings. I knew my own mother had been late to count-less events because she had been digging through her cav-ernous jewelry box hunting for an ear-ring. But if it turned out that Pam, my friend the massage therapist, and I were the only two women in Chicago driven crazy every day by

One of my *Shark Tank* deals from Season Four, the Drop Stop "Boyz," as they jokingly want me to call them, came up with a creative way to conduct their research without people even knowing it. They would install the Drop Stop into people's cars and tell them that something had been placed there that was eighteen inches long and in plain view, and give them five minutes to find it. When they couldn't, the "Boyz" would take their keys, drop them on the Drop Stop, and observe. People's reaction was so excited and positive that the inventors knew they were on to something great.

our ineffective jewelry boxes, I wanted to know immediately, not after sinking my life savings into a product no one wanted.

So as soon as my prototype was complete, I visited as many of Chicago's socioeconomically diverse areas as I could, and I asked people to fill out my marketing questionnaire, look at my earring organizer, and tell me if they would buy it. I started out right in front of the beautiful Fourth Presbyterian Church on Michigan Avenue, across from the John Hancock Building. Why a church? Michigan Avenue is like Fifth Avenue in New York City or Rodeo

Drive in Los Angeles—it's not the kind of neighborhood where retailers take kindly to people sitting anywhere near their storefronts. But it does attract a wide array of shoppers and tourists from all over the world. I needed to be there. I chose to sit in front of a church because I thought a church might not shoo me away or call the police to report me for loitering. A church kind of has to be nice to you.

I discreetly parked myself at a little table in a small corner at the front of the building, my organizer hidden beneath a small piece of black fabric. I'd carefully approach every woman who passed by with a huge smile on my face and ask if she could take five minutes to answer a questionnaire about a really cool new earring organizer. "And look," I'd say, "I'll give you this pen if you'll give me five minutes!" like it was the greatest gift in the world. People would generally laugh. That small gesture would often break the ice. I probably got about 75 percent of the people I approached this way to talk to me and answer my questions. If you're fun and jovial, people won't find you threatening.

Every time I showed my invention to a stranger when doing my market research, it would cross my mind that there was the possibility that person could steal my idea. But I knew I didn't have a choice. You probably have the same reservations. But you can't live in fear. Fear can be paralyzing, and if you're not always moving forward, you might as well give up now. I didn't have a choice back then, and neither do you. If you don't let anyone see your product, you can't get the information you need. So just be careful. Let people handle your invention and give you their honest opinions. Keep your product under wraps, literally, if you can, as I did by hiding my organizer under black fabric unless a woman had it in her hands. It will work to your advantage. There's no better way to pique people's curiosity than to offer them a chance to see something no one else is allowed to see. Take every step you can to protect yourself and still get the information you need. And whatever you do, do not allow anyone to take pictures!

I performed my routine hundreds of times on Michigan Avenue, from sunup to sundown. Maybe a day or so later I headed to a shopping mall on the west side of Chicago. The day after that, I was approaching women at a mall on the South Side. And the next day, I was at a mall on the North Side. In less than a week I presented my product to every socioeconomic demographic the city had to offer. I also hit the Taste of Chicago, the biggest food festival in the world, where hundreds of restaurants set up booths for people to taste their preparations. It's a huge city event that attracts an enormous cross section of people, and it was the perfect place for me to canvass potential customers.

> Sometimes if you expose your idea too soon and too widely, you risk losing it. Conversely, sometimes people are so afraid to reveal their ideas that they sit on them and don't get anywhere. Strike a careful balance between the two extremes.

Unfortunately, booths for the event had to be reserved months ahead of time. Normally I'm very legal eagle and big on following the rules. But six months earlier I didn't have an idea for an earring organizer or the need for a booth, and now I did, and this was too good an opportunity to miss. So I snuck in. There was a little section at the end of the fair set up for local artisans to showcase their wares. I asked some of the jewelry makers if I could sit between them and display their earrings on my organizer. I would help them push their jewelry while people filled out my questionnaire. It was a perfect symbiotic relationship. I helped increase these artists' sales by drawing attention to their earrings, and they helped me demonstrate how useful my product was and get my questionnaire answered. I probably sat there for two or three hours before the police finally came and shooed me away because I didn't have an official booth. They were right to do so, of course. By then, though, I had gotten all the information I needed anyway. And my information told me that this organizer was going to be on every jewelry-lover's wish list. My gut had always told me this invention was a hero, and now I had the closest thing I'd ever have as proof until it went on sale.

TIPS

1. If people criticize your design or otherwise offer a critique, don't argue back. Don't try to convince them that their initial reaction is wrong. Listen, take notes, and pay attention to patterns. You'll never please everyone, but if you go out there and hear a resounding and consistent "No," pay attention. Be grateful you're able to find out now that no one wants or understands your invention, not after you've got units sitting on the shelves gathering dust. If, on the other hand, you get enthusiastic responses like, "Wow, I wish I'd thought of that," or, "I would definitely buy that," that tells you people are excited by your idea and are likely to buy it.

2. The percentage of reviews that need to be positive in order for you to trust your data depends on your product. If you're selling something brand-new, you want to see an approval rating between 60 and 70 percent. This means that your concept has resonated with the population. But if you're simply adding a new option to

a competitive market, your numbers don't have to be quite as high. Apple's iPhone has 14 percent of the U.S. mobile market. Fourteen percent wouldn't be a great number if Apple were only competing against one other mobile company, but given how much competition there is for market share, 14 percent is still a lot of units being sold. No one can say the iPhone isn't working.

3. Use this time to understand your product and hone your pitch. Before you show your product, you should have all your top-selling features down cold: (a) what problem your invention solves, (b) how it works, and (c) why your consumer needs it. Once your product is sitting on a shelf, your packaging will answer those questions for you, but when you're showing it to people, you need to present it in such a way that consumers quickly understand its qualities and whether they would use it. If it's hard to explain now, no one is going to get it when it's sitting on the shelf without you, either.

You need to be able to communicate the kernel of your idea quickly. If you find yourself making long-winded presentations, people won't understand; or if you have to explain things more than once, or if people are staring at you confused and bewildered, your product probably isn't a hero.

4. You want to make a neutral presentation of the facts. You're not trying to convince people to like your inven-

tion; you want them to come to the conclusion that it's terrific on their own. You don't want to pressure people to give you the answer they think you want to hear. When you're speaking to people about your invention, just outline what the product is and what it does, and observe your consumers' reactions. Watch them handle your product. Read their eyes, if you can. Does it make them smile? Do their brows furrow? Do they press it into their friends' hands so they can try it, too? All of this information is useful.

5. The way you ask questions matters. Sometimes when I would ask people whether they liked the organizer or thought it was cool, the answer would be an emphatic yes, but when I pressed forward and asked whether they would *buy* the organizer, if they said no it was usually because they didn't like having anything on their dresser or countertop. So sometimes if people say yes it's because they like something, so it's smart to ask another question that digs deeper, such as whether they would purchase it, and if not, why? It helps you gain a better and broader perspective of your product and consumer.

Now, what people say and how people behave don't always necessarily line up. Your market research can't guarantee sales; all it can do is give you a fairly good idea of how consumers feel in general and at first flush about your product. You can use your market research to figure out your best strategy and determine whether people will want to buy your product, but you can't count on the results 100 percent.

Often, your product's performance in the market will take

you completely by surprise. When I did my own research, overwhelmingly the majority of women I approached who said they liked jewelry also said they would buy the organizer. Yet in the areas where people most said they'd buy it is where the organizer sold the least, while where consumers said they'd least buy it is where it sold in retailers the most. This is an excellent time to be testing, analyzing, and questioning your product and your sales strategy from every angle so that you can address any issues well before you start to pitch retailers, or place an order with your manufacturer. The sooner you figure out the flaws or weaknesses and fix them, the better.

At the end of your market research, you should be able to answer the following:

1. The percentage of people who liked my product: _____
   The percentage who did not like it: _____
   The percentage who were neutral: _____
2. The percentage of people who felt my product was something they wanted: _____
   The percentage of people who felt it was something they needed:_____
3. The percentage of people who said they would buy it:_____
4. Overall, consumers said they would pay between _____ and _____ for the product.
5. Where they said they would expect to find it:_____

Quantifying your feedback forces you to objectively weigh the likelihood of your product's success on the market.

PRICING YOUR PRODUCT

A word of caution: Often inventors go overboard, trying to add as many bells and whistles to their product as possible, and then find themselves priced out of the market because all of those whistles made it too expensive to produce.

Pricing is tricky. In fact, big companies often hire huge consulting firms to research the ideal prices for their products. Major brands raise and lower their product prices all the time to see how the changes affect their market share. The results can be eye-opening. Often, you'd think the cheapest laundry detergent would sell the best, but when you mix in the effects of marketing campaigns and brand loyalty, that's not always the case. Prices fluctuate regionally, too. On the East Coast, the highest priced detergent may be the same one that is the lowest priced on the West Coast.

I have a friend with a vineyard who actually raised his prices so his wines would be some of the most expensive on the market, and they then started selling better. The competition at the lower end of the market was just too fierce to break in. So, pricing strategies can be crazy and really interesting. When your business gets huge, you'll have to learn about pricing strategies in detail, or you'll hear about it from your wholesale customers when they say your sales aren't pacing with where they need to be. As a new small business, however, you'll start with the basics.

To me, the pricing basics break down to a simple three-pronged approach that relates to three key bits of information:

Cost to manufacture and distribute
Competition
Gut feeling

1. Consider Your Cost

First, you have to know your manufacturing, labor, and operating costs: how much it costs to make and distribute your item. This number is not limited to just what you pay a factory for each part; you need to add in the cost of packaging and some overhead for the trucking (if produced locally), shipping (if produced overseas), storage, and systems involved to account for it or the EDI (electronic data interchange) that must be established if you're going to do business with big retailers. Make sure to also include any sales or rep commissions, if you have to pay them. Don't forget the instruction sheets you have to include with the product (they typically only cost a few cents, but that's still a cost). What is your overhead? And how much do you plan to spend on marketing? (Hint: not much. See Chapter 11.) Some costs will be fixed, like rent, which doesn't change from month to month, and some costs will be variable, like your monthly utilities. Other costs will fluctuate based on your production levels at any one time.

Your cost calculation should look like this:

$$\text{Materials} + \text{labor} + \text{overhead} + \text{transportation} = \text{total product cost.}$$

After you total your costs, add on an acceptable profit margin, which establishes how much profit you're going to earn. For example, if your product's total costs were $6, and you added on a profit margin of $4, which would translate to a 40 percent margin, you could price your product at a $10 wholesale cost.

($6) Total product cost + ($4) desired profit margin = $10 wholesale cost.

Then you need to know how much your wholesale customers mark up their items so you know how much profit *they* want to make when they sell your invention. Each store works on a different margin and even within a store, different product categories have different required margins. Typically, items with high return rates like clothing have higher margin needs than do consumables like soap and paper towels. Many stores set their prices by "keystoning" the wholesale cost, meaning they double it. So if you sell to them at $10, they will sell it to the consumer for $20, which is a 50 percent margin. Other stores might sell the same product for $12.99, which is a 23 percent margin, and others may sell it for as high as $32.99, for a 70 percent margin.

You need to determine which stores you're going to sell to in order to know what margin to use. For this example, let's say you are going to sell to local boutiques that typically use 50 percent as their margin. That would mean that if you suggest the stores retail it at $19.99, you need to be able to sell it to them for $10. In our example, at a $6 cost and a $4 margin, this pricing allows you a comfortable profit.

Note: In this example there are no freight costs. However, there may be some fine-tuning of your wholesale costs to your retailer to allow them to account for their freight in (what they pay to truck your product to their locations) and any extra charges they incur.

Wholesale cost to store + freight in/ (1 - store margin) = retail price.

Using the example, this becomes: $10 + 0/.50 = $19.99.

Do your research and familiarize yourself with each retail customer you want to sell to. Understand all you can about them and how they operate. The more knowledgeable you are, the more appealing you become. Buyers like to work with people who know what they are doing.

2. Consider Your Competition

You need to scout out your competition. Competition should be viewed as anything else in the marketplace that solves the same problem as your product. If you don't have a direct competitor, examine the prices of other products that fall into your category. You're going to walk a fine line. What do their products retail at in your target stores? If yours is priced much higher or much lower than theirs, you could be at a disadvantage unless you can offer a good reason for the price difference. What features or benefits does yours have or not have that theirs do? If they are priced less than your product is calculating out to be, can your packaging or marketing overcome the difference? If your price is significantly less than theirs, maybe you can raise your price.

A lot of new businesses will try to sell for cheaper than the competitor, believing that new customers will automatically gravitate toward a new brand if it is less expensive. That's not necessarily true, because perception is everything. Also, brand loyalty is a powerful thing. On the other hand, if your product is priced a lot higher than the competition's, you may have to lower your margin expectations or rethink how or where you make your product to trim costs. You have to anticipate what will happen to your product's sales if you place it at its current price right next to your competition at its higher or lower price. That's where your gut comes in.

3. Pay Attention to Your Gut

What does your gut tell you? I don't employ those big consulting firms to study my pricing and give me price-range impact studies and elasticity reports. It helps that I have quite a few years selling products in a lot of categories, but I basically trust my gut as a consumer. It comes down to a basic feeling: what is this worth to the average consumer, and how badly do they need it? I imagine my product sitting on the shelf or shown on the TV screen with a range of prices under it. When I see one that makes me want to jump off my seat and pick up a phone to call in my order, or I imagine reaching out to grab the item, I go for that price. (My gut told me that my earring organizer needed to be under $20.) If my gut price is about the same as the target selling price I calculated, I know I'm almost there. If it is not, I know I need to look for another supplier or even possibly lower my margin expectations.

MAGIC PRICE POINTS

Magic price points are $9.99, $14.99, $19.99, $24.99, $29.99, and so on. Hitting the magic price point is key to getting people to reach for your product. If your pricing calculates to $20.73, do all you can to get it to $19.99. Psychologically, it is so much easier for a customer to reach for a $19.99 item than for an "over $20 item." On the flip side, if your item is calculating out to $23.32, think about rounding up to $24.99. Customers won't see the $1.67 difference as a bargain, really, and may actually think the $24.99 price has a higher perceived value. Of course, competition and your ultimate margin have to be taken into account before you make your final decision.

Then again, I sometimes find that despite the fact that a

product is superior to other options out there, people won't pay the extra couple of dollars for it. When they know that there is something else out there a little bit cheaper that will do the same thing, the majority will buy the cheaper one—unless you can offer brand status or a clear benefit over the other item. I once made an umbrella that looked and functioned much better than anything else on the market, but I discovered that the majority of people would rather spend $10 over and over for cheapie umbrellas than buy a superior umbrella for $20—and so the product failed.

About being the highest priced item: As you know by now, my ultimate goal has always been to bring people a great product at the best value, and I aim for the biggest, broadest market. Sometimes, though, you may find that your product is overengineered or really high quality, which can make the price much higher than the competition that is selling the hell out of it. The question is not whether people will pay the extra cost for a better item versus the alternatives out there. Rather, it is how many people will pay the extra cost for the better product? You don't see a lot of Ferraris out on the streets, but that doesn't mean that the carmaker isn't rolling in profits.

DON'T BE GREEDY

Some people use the same "keystone" strategy as retailers, meaning they calculate their profit by doubling their costs, and they don't want to sell for anything less. But you will need to balance your needs and the needs of your family against what the general public will be willing to pay for your product. You may not be able to earn a 50 percent markup and still price your product competitively. Sometimes you can make only a 30 percent margin, sometimes only 40 percent. Evaluate each item individually.

Not long ago, I met the father of a young entrepreneur, eleven-year-old Lukas Pakter. He was so proud of his son, who wanted to be an entrepreneur and started his first enterprise, selling glow sticks. As you can see, this kid already has better sense than many of his older, greedier competitors. Lukas wrote his story to me in his own words:

> So it all started 2 years ago at a 4th of July festival. There was a man selling little rings that would fit on your fingers and glow all different colors. I remember him selling them for about 4 dollars, which seemed really overpriced. The next morning I looked up how much the little rings cost and they cost only about 50 cents each, so everyone was getting ripped off. Two years later, I was looking for a way to make some money and I came up with the idea to get 200 glow wristbands, which cost 40 dollars, and then I also bought 100 glow necklaces for 20 dollars. At the 4th of July, I sold the wristbands for 1 dollar each and the necklaces for 2 dollars each, which to me and the people who bought them seemed like a more reasonable price than the price the guy was charging 2 years ago . . . . I couldn't carry all 300 glow bracelets and necklaces, so my stepbrother Diesel handed out the glow sticks and I took care of the money . . . . By the end of the day I had made a profit of about 300 dollars. I split the 300 dollars with Diesel.

Lukas is already way ahead of many entrepreneurs because he's smart enough not to be greedy. That's a lesson I'm constantly trying to impress on people. Set your price correctly, and you will make plenty of money. Don't be a one-and-done because you were so set on making a 50 percent margin that you set the price too high on your product and made it fail.

My strategy has always been to make a good-quality product at an affordable price so that everyone can enjoy my products. That means I sell at the lowest price I can afford to, taking slimmer margins but hoping for bigger volume. My theory is that the more volume you sell, the more consumers have your product (which lends itself to more word-of-mouth sales), the happier retailers are, and the longer you stay on the shelf—or additionally in my case, on QVC. It's a simple theory and it works. Sometimes when I can, I can make a better margin on a low-cost item, but I'll have to take a lower margin on a different higher-priced item. It makes more sense to sell a product at the right price than to get stuck with inventory because consumers think it's too expensive. Pricing according to what feels right for the market, and what people tell you they would pay for it, is the smartest way to go.

THE TRUTH IS THAT THESE days I don't do much market research. One of my strengths has always been that I have good gut instincts about what people want and what people will buy. But it also helps that I have relationships with some of the most astute buyers in the business. As I'm developing and testing products, I can often count on the buyers at QVC or in retail to share their thoughts with me. They have tons of experience with what works and what fails.

Sometimes you need to convince them that your product is

different from or better than something they might have seen in the past that didn't work. That's what happened with my closet organizer. The buyers said they'd tried closet organizers before and they didn't sell. I needed to convince them to give mine a chance. I said mine was different—it spins and has shoe pockets on all three sides and has purse slots. I had to be really persuasive, and was excited when they finally said they'd give it a try. Fortunately the product became a great seller, and over the years we sold hundreds of thousands of units in varying styles and configurations. They're still on QVC today.

Still, I'm always grateful for these buyers' opinions and I value their input. Many times they have brought great thoughts and ideas for product enhancements to the table. It's a good thing I have them as my sounding board. My team also has great input and ideas. It's always a team effort. One funny running joke among all of us is that Dan, who is unbelievably brilliant in so many ways, and a whiz with numbers, is not naturally a "product guy." No matter what new product I'm coming up with, his initial reaction is, "Nope, not gonna work. No one's gonna buy it. Not gonna work." "Yes, it will work. Don't worry, they will buy it," I'll tell him. "Trust me. I have a little bit of a track record. Just watch." Everyone at the table will crack up. Dan's a good sport. He sees us laughing and he knows why. The product will go on to sell millions. And yet no matter how many times we've repeated this scenario, he still feels compelled to be the skeptic. We all have our areas of expertise. Dan is a numbers guy; I'm the inventor. That's why we're a perfect team.

> **Surround yourself with people who have different skills than you. Everyone benefits from complementary skills.**

I certainly don't have a perfect

record. Market research might have saved me
from one item that didn't work at all—a smartphone wallet. It looked kind of like a knapsack
for your cell phone. It was a black leather case
that adhered to the back of your phone with a

> **"Your best teacher is your last mistake."**
>
> –AUTHOR UNKNOWN

hook and loop fastener (like Velcro) and had a secure, slim, and seal-
able pocket at the top where you could put your credit cards, a little
cash, and ID. My friend Jeff brought the idea to me. I didn't create it,
but I loved it! I thought it was brilliant, and was perfect for someone
like me who doesn't like to carry the extra weight of a wallet.

I thought it would be perfect for other women, too. A woman
may leave her purse at home, but she will not go out without her
phone. But where to put your ID and a little cash or a credit card if
you don't want to schlep around a handbag? The smartphone wallet solved that problem. I loved it (I still use mine). But it didn't
sell. It was only later that I asked around and discovered that a lot
of people didn't want to put Velcro on their smartphones. Jeff was
definitely on to something, because today many cases have inte-
grated slots for credit cards. I just wanted something that could
hold more—but I guess the market didn't. I always learn from
every experience.

Some people feel better knowing they've done the research
for every product, even when they have a proven track record.
Others have a knack for hitting the sweet spots and don't feel the
need to dig so deep every time. Continue to do market research
before introducing new products until you have a track record of
success and feel you have honed your instincts. Eventually, you
will find that you need a lot less market research once your business is up and running, especially if you take the advice I offer
later in this book, and create extensions off the product lines
you've already created.

MARKET RESEARCH
TO-DO LIST:

☐ Write a questionnaire complete with 8–10 open-ended questions that will elicit honest feedback.

☐ Identify a minimum of three locations for face-to-face consumer research.

☐ Identify online sites for research.

☐ Establish that people like your product.

☐ Establish that there is a demand for your product.

☐ Establish that people will buy your product.

☐ Have a good idea of what the market will bear.

☐ Set a suggested retail price.

5

HOW TO GET FUNDING

*"All of our dreams can come true if we have
the courage to pursue them."*

—WALT DISNEY

INVENTING YOUR WAY TO SUCCESS AND WEALTH DOESN'T COME
cheap. Maybe you started working out of your garage and built
your first model out of odds and ends at home, but once you
decide to move from occasional hobbyist to full-time entrepreneur, you'll be amazed at how much money you'll spend before
you even make your first pitch. First, there's the money you'll
spend on your prototype. Then, once your market research con-
firms there is interest and demand for your invention, you'll need
to start spending money to manufacture your product. You may
also file a patent, which can sometimes be another hefty investment.

Together these expenditures can add up to anywhere from a
few thousand dollars to tens of thousands of dollars, and that's
before a single unit has been made. And chances are you didn't

think to start a fund ahead of time to finance this endeavor. How could you? If you're like most people, your great idea hit you like a bolt out of the blue. And once you recognized its potential, you also realized that you would have to move lightning fast if you wanted to ensure that no one beat you to it. So now you suddenly need cash, and lots of it. Unless you've already built and sold a business, or are otherwise in an extremely comfortable financial position, you're probably going to have to borrow money to follow through with getting your invention to market.

How much will you need? The best way to figure that out is to draw up a solid business plan. This is where you put into writing a detailed explanation of what your business is, how it will operate, and how you intend to make it grow. If you've gotten this far, you've probably already gathered a lot of the information you need. The market research you've completed to determine your invention's market demand, competition, customer demographics, and price will be the foundation for your plan.

In contrast to your elevator pitch, which boils your idea or business down to a couple of sentences that can explain and excite even a stranger about your idea, a business plan is a very detailed document. It's required if you're going to ask a bank or venture capital (VC) firm for money, but it should be written even if you are going to self-fund your company. You'll learn a lot by doing it, and it is something to follow when times get tough. You can and should even publish it for your key employees so you know everyone is on the same page.

A *business plan* is a multi-page document that should explain to an investor or stranger who has no prior knowledge of your product or business exactly what your product or service is, how and where you are going to make it, how you're going to sell it, your assessment of the competition and why yours is better, and how much money you are going to need to start it and run it in the near and long term. Each type of business is different, but for a basic product-invention business, these are the minimums:

1. Executive Summary (1–2 paragraphs)

2. Company Summary (1 paragraph)

3. Market Description (1 paragraph)

4. Products (1 paragraph)

5. Manufacturing or Procurement (1 paragraph).

6. Sales Strategy (1 paragraph)

7. Fulfillment (1 paragraph)

8. Marketing and PR Campaign (1 paragraph)

9. Management Team (1 paragraph)

10. Patent and Trademarks (1 paragraph)

11. Sales Projections (1 page)

12. Operating Costs (1 page)

13. Five-Year Projected Financial Statements including a Breakeven Analysis (1–2 pages)

14. Launch, Inventory, and First Steps (1 page)

15. Financing—Equity Offering and/or Loans
    (1 paragraph)

16. Investment Opportunity (1 paragraph)

After reading your business plan, investors don't have to be convinced to invest or not. They should understand the concept and be informed enough about the key issues and assumption that they can go out and research the parts they are concerned about on their own and come back to you for answers to their most important questions. Your management team should have a clear understanding of the goals and milestones they should be working toward.

Once you prepare your business plan, don't just shelve it. You should update it often, even if you are the only employee. It will make you realize when you've missed deadlines and have overspent. It will remind you if you've gotten off track in your day-to-day operations, or have changed your focus, so you can decide if that is really a good or bad thing. If you did get investors, they will be expecting you to be following that original plan when it comes time for a board meeting. If you decide a course change is really for the best, they are going to need convincing; the updated business plan is about all that will give them confidence that you know what you're doing and not just chasing the flavor of the month.

> Putting together the business plan will ensure that you know your business inside and out, and you will be fully prepared for any questions a potential investor or lender might ask. These questions will differ across categories.

The main problem I often see in young entrepreneurs' business plans is that they are naïve. They don't understand the difference between a great idea and a great business. They write a business plan using all the information they have, but they fail to take into account the information they don't have, meaning they don't look far enough ahead and plan for the cost of growth. For example, entrepreneurs will usually know what it will cost to make their products, and what they will sell them for. They know their margins and use that number to calculate their profits based on how many units they can sell. They know which stores they are going to try to sell to, they predict that store sales will double or triple, and from those numbers they calculate their worth.

The problem is that these inventors completely forget that those additional sales are going to require additional infrastructure, like real estate and staff, especially if they land Walmart as a client. They don't take into account the cost of all those adjustments. Additional sales also bring more risk of being stuck with overhead when things go slow or bad. You need to plan for that, too. Nothing sells forever, and sometimes items are a flash in the pan. Entrepreneurs tend to plot their sales in a continuing upward curve, ignoring the fact that even hugely popular products will see that that upward arc can eventually plateau, and then begin to fall.

So a good business plan should include some thought to how you're going to keep the business growing through product extensions and new ideas. New ideas are the lifeblood of a business. Investors will love to hear about your great idea, and they love revolutionary concepts, but when they're looking at your business plan, they're looking for evidence that your business can survive beyond your single great idea. If they don't see it, they know that if they want to invest in something that can make them some money for the long term, they're going to have to step in and help build the business themselves, using their own knowledge, connections, and infrastructure. So your business plan not only serves as your guide to keeping your business on track, it is the document that investors will read to determine whether you're someone who is going to make them money or someone who is going to lose their money. Your business plan needs to indicate that you have thought ahead about all the potential costs for running a business, not just selling an idea.

There is no one-size-fits-all business plan; every business is different and thus has different necessary components and cash needs. But the reality is that at this stage you simply can't know for sure how much money you're going to need. Even the best planning and organizational skills can't protect you from the unexpected, and there will inevitably be times when you have to back up and start over or head down another path. Whenever that happens, it will cost you time and materials, which of course means it will cost you money. Few entrepreneurs (no one I know) have ever come in under or exactly on budget. Every first-time entrepreneur has to learn along the way.

BUDGET FOR UNEXPECTED EXPENSES

Revisions

Very few prototypes are perfect on the first try. You'll make an adjustment, and solve one problem and inadvertently create another. Your changes may double the cost of your sample. There goes money down the drain. I've had it happen to me.

Excessive Shipping Charges

To keep costs down, many inventors have their inventions, including their prototypes, made in Asia. But the cost of shipping samples back and forth between here and China can cost three or four hundred dollars per package, depending on the weight and volume of your product. Of course, the more samples you send back and forth as you make adjustments, the higher the costs.

Compliance Issues

You need to be aware of government regulations and consumer product safety laws. If you manufacture your product and it fails to meet certain requirements, you'll have to scrap your inventory and start anew.

The consequences for putting out a product that fails to comply can include everything from paying a fine to, in the worst-case scenario, its being recalled. It would be exceedingly difficult for a new entrepreneur to recover from a recall because not only would the entrepreneur lose a ton of money, it would hurt all of his or her relationships with retailers and customers.

Repacking and Reworking

Let's say you've redesigned your packaging, or you've had to fix a design flaw on a product that you've already manufactured and it is sitting in a storage facility. It can cost tens of thousands of dollars to pay someone to empty each package, fix the product if necessary, put it in a new package, then put it into the master cartons (giant boxes that hold multiple units for shipping). It's called *reworking*, and it's a service often offered by the fulfillment centers many young businesses work with to store and ship orders.

For this reason, once you have established your budget with all contingencies, add another 5 to 10 percent to it and call it the "Stuff Happens" account. Murphy's law states that anything that can go wrong will go wrong. I like to add the following caveat: anything that can go wrong, will go wrong, unless you stay on top of every aspect of your business and are prepared to jump in to solve problems immediately.

The more investors can see that you've looked at your business from every angle, and have a strategic and financial plan in place to deal with shifts in the market, glitches, changes in regulations, and any other potential pitfalls, the more they will feel confident that their money will be well spent and that they will be supporting a successful venture. But of course, there will always be instances where something inopportune occurs that you simply could not foresee.

Overspending on Image

You need to be responsible and frugal, and wise. When starting out, you don't need a fancy office, or staff, or anything other than the bare bones of what you need to get the job done. Companies offer perks to their employees because they have to make them happy, productive, and loyal. Your perk is that you don't work for anyone but yourself anymore, and if you haven't already quit your day job, this invention will (you hope) allow you to do so. You don't get a comfortable office, summer Fridays, or gourmet snacks. You can have those wonderful things later. Better yet, you can have that for yourself and your employees later, when you've grown your business and are reaping the profits. But right now, do without as much as possible.

Unfortunately, if there is one piece of conventional wisdom that is true, it's this: you've got to spend money to make money. However, you should, at all costs, avoid using up your nest egg or that of your parents, or of leveraging your home. It's worth it to take on partners with greater financial resources or clout, if necessary. Even if they don't come through with all the money you need, their credit worthiness or status in the business community can help immensely as you round up funds.

VALUING YOUR BUSINESS

One of the first things you hear on every *Shark Tank* episode is how much money the entrepreneur wants and how much equity he or she is willing to give up for it. For instance, the entrepreneur might ask for $50,000 for 10 percent of the company. All the sharks quickly jot down these numbers and do a calculation. We take the money asked for and divide it by the percent of the business offered.

$$\$50,000 \, / \, .10 = \$500,000.$$

The entrepreneur is telling us that he or she believes the company is worth $500,000.

Now it's up to us to decide if it really is. Confession: I hate math. I can make calculations in my head, but not always as fast as I need to on the show. The producers don't let us take our phones or even a calculator on the set with us, so I use a little Excel cheat sheet. It's a big chart that lists possible "Asks" down the first column and all the different percentages across the top row. It comes in very handy when I need to calculate quickly.

What's a Business Worth?

You'll hear my fellow shark Kevin O'Leary often mention that the "multiple" on some type of business is "five times free cash flow" or "one times sales." In simple terms, a venture capital (VC) multiple calculates how much a business is worth based on a number of years of the business's future projected income. When he says "five times free cash flow," he means he wants to see an earnings line that produces enough excess cash that his initial investment is paid back in five years. What he's really asking is, "When do I get my money back?" (That's another frequent Kevin line.)

You'll hear Mark Cuban make fun of Kevin for applying a VC multiple to the *Shark Tank* businesses. I agree. You can't use a multiple on a brand-new business or start-up. You need to have a few years of history before you can really start applying broad ratios. But the concept is good to understand, because most of the people you ask for money are going to be coming from this type of background. I basically want to see my money come back in one to three years.

What do I look at when valuing a business? First, I look at the product or idea, and I gauge whether it's unique and interesting. Do I feel this is something that will sell well? Can I help make it sell well? If yes, I look at the entrepreneur's manufacturing costs to determine whether the item can sell for a good price that will motivate people to buy. If the answer to that is yes as well, then I think about all my distribution channels (for example, QVC, department stores, Bed Bath & Beyond, Walmart, Costco, drugstores, grocery stores, and so on) and how many would sell to each. If it looks like in one year it can produce more profits than my investment, I'm basically in.

As I said, I don't even *think* about valuing the business until after we get some proven sales history and momentum going. To be fair to Kevin, though, all the sharks are thinking, "When do I get my money back?"

RAISING CAPITAL

There are many ways to get money for your product, but the safest way is to use your own money as wisely as possible. Often, however, even inventors who operate with the frugality of Scrooge just can't carry their invention all the way to production. So with or without partners, where do inventors turn to raise the capital to fund their dreams?

Family and Friends

Family is probably the easiest source of money for new entrepreneurs. It is wonderful if you have family members who can offer not only emotional support as you embark on your new endeavors but financial support as well. However, though family is often the first place people turn for a loan, it's also one of the riskiest. Be extremely careful in how you set up your arrangement. It may be best not to formalize the loan details to anything more than an agreed-upon financial amount and interest rate, which is required by the IRS for any loan over $10,000. Without that stated interest rate, the loan will be considered a gift, sticking your family member with a gift tax at the end of the year. Regardless, any family member who loans money to another family member should, for all intents and purposes, treat the loan as a gift.

So, take the expectation and pressure of a specific repayment date out of the equation by drafting a contract that states, "Repayment will occur when the business starts producing net income and the company has greater than three months' cash to keep its inventory and liabilities paid." Yes, it's possible that the business will never earn that much money. Yes, this is still the best kind of financial agreement between family members.

Many experts will disagree strongly with this advice, however. They will say that every detail of the loan and repayment schedule should be established ahead of time, and that lenders should have a reasonable expectation of getting their money back by a certain date, even if you're not earning a profit. But I don't believe any family member should loan any money with the expectation of getting it back. The family member can *hope* to get it back, but should give it with the understanding that it's entirely possible that won't happen. And I'm not the only one who feels this way. When he was interviewed for *Time* magazine after being nominated 1999 Person of the Year, Jeff Bezos admitted that he said as much when he solicited investments from his friends and family to fund his crazy idea for a new thing called Amazon: "I think there's a 70 percent chance you're going to lose all your money, so don't invest unless you can afford to lose it."

You should insist that if family members cannot loan their money with that attitude, they shouldn't lend it at all. It's the only way to guarantee that your relationships will not suffer if, for any reason your business doesn't succeed the way you think it will, or at least as fast as you think it will. If you draft an airtight legal lending document, and the borrower fails to honor the agreement and repay at the promised time, the only recourse a lender has to make sure he gets his money back is to sue. Is that really something either of you is prepared to face? It is a tragedy when a family tears itself apart over money, yet it happens all the time. If you think there is any possibility that your relationship with a family member could be damaged should your business not succeed, or you find yourself unable to repay the loan in a timely manner, do not take the money. But if you do, make sure your agreement establishes in writing what will happen if you succeed and what will happen if you don't succeed. Ensure that no one can say he or she wasn't warned.

In the event you feel you simply must draft a more formal loan agreement, you might consider going to a bank, applying for a loan, and having a family member put up a CD (Certificate of Deposit) as collateral. Let the bank give you the money directly rather than to your family member. If you default, and the bank cannot satisfy the outstanding balance from your business, only then will the bank go to the CD for the balance. In the meantime, the person's money is gaining interest and any funds taken to satisfy your loan can be treated as a business loss for tax purposes. This will reduce the family member's personal loss by offsetting future income taxes.

This advice goes for borrowing money from friends, as well. Often, you can get a group of your friends excited about getting in on your big idea, and you can raise some capital by consolidating small amounts of money from each of them. But if you take money from friends, try to set your agreement up without specifying a repayment due date, the same as you would with a family loan. Tell your friends up front that you are asking them to take a risk,

Make sure everyone's expectations are the same, and are documented to avoid problems later. Worse than your business failing is losing a friend or family member along with it.

and that you'll do everything you can to pay them back, but in the event you cannot repay, they have to be able to absorb the loss and still maintain their friendship with you. Then document your agreement so that everyone has something to refer to in the future.

If you just cannot raise the funds from your friends in this manner, you may be forced to offer some equity in the form of a convertible note. This means that if you do not repay the loan within a certain amount of time, the lender has the option to convert it into equity shares in your company. You'll need to get advice on how to draft this kind of loan, but your goal should always be to give away as little equity as possible. Give away too much now, and you could face big problems later when you try to get more money. Don't be the person who allocated 50 percent of his business to a group of friends in exchange for a $500 loan. In addition, the share conversion value should be tied to

> Try to avoid allocating any equity in this early stage of raising money. It can significantly impact you later on if the business is a success and you need to raise large amounts of money.

the business value at the time of conversion, not the date of the loan, so that you don't end up giving half of your business away for a very small amount of money that you might have needed when you were desperate.

Banks

If you've got good credit and your business looks good on paper, you may be able to get a small business loan from a bank. Typically, though, a bank loan will require collateral. Be careful when negotiating a bank loan, and make sure you aren't taking such a high risk that you could wind up losing something you can't live without, like your house.

The best time to get a bank loan is after you have gotten your first purchase orders. Scrape together just enough money to get you to that point from other sources, then go to the bank and use your purchase orders as collateral. Once you have purchase orders, the bank will see that you're credible and will be more likely to believe that you will be able to pay it back. Bank loans will typically involve a higher interest rate than anything you would negotiate with friends or family, but this additional cost is probably worth it if it helps you launch your business and makes you beholden to a neutral party rather than someone whose relationship matters to you.

I had always known that I would have to take out a loan to make my organizer. I had about $25,000 of my own money that I could use to get the prototype made and to pay for various expenses such as traveling to make pitches; but like most entrepreneurs, I couldn't cover the manufacturing and packaging costs on my own. As you'll recall, I got a $120,000 quote to make the tools for my organizer. By the time I found out that number, I knew I had orders coming in (more on how that happened later). So, to determine how much I'd need to borrow from the bank, I had to calculate how much it would cost to create inventory, hire a graphic designer, get packaging made, and pay for all the other expenses that would surely arise. Ultimately, I got a $300,000 line of credit, and I ended up drawing out a total of $250,000, which covered the following:

Do everything you can to maintain a personal relationship with your banker. Make all your interest payments on time, and when possible, keep your banker informed of your seasonality or low and high cash periods. Doing this won't guarantee that you'll get a little leniency should the maturity date come and you're not flush enough to pay, but you never know—it might make your banker willing to work with you to buy you some time. Remember, the bank is a business, too. Often, no matter how good the prospects look for your company, if you haven't paid your debt, the bank will grab whatever assets you have at that moment, cut their losses, and move on. Building a good relationship with your banker— just as with anyone else with whom you do business—can only help if you ever find yourself with your back against the wall.

$120,000 for tools
$5,000 for graphic design and photography
$25,000 for packaging
$100,000 for a first run of 20,000 units

These numbers would probably be slightly different today, and may not even be applicable for your particular product, but one thing is still true: once your orders start coming in, it's amazing how fast the money starts going out. Fortunately, once I was up and running I was able to use the profits from my first orders to fund the business. Larger orders allowed me to get better terms from our suppliers—for example, instead of having to pay half up front and half on delivery, we were able to negotiate payment due thirty days after delivery. I was also able to increase my credit line so I could accommodate more customers. As I started getting mega orders from QVC, our credit line expanded quickly to about $5 million.

Government SBA Loans

Loans are available from banks or institutions that have been backed by the U.S. government's Small Business Administration (SBA). Basically, the SBA puts up collateral for different kinds of loans ranging from general loans to be used for establishing your business or growing it, to microloans for smaller sums of money, to 504 loans that can be used to purchase long-term machinery and equipment. Applicants are required to meet different SBA criteria, depending on what loan is desired. Visit www.sba.gov to find out more about applying for a government loan.

Venture Capital Firms

If you are denied a bank loan, the next place to turn may be a venture capital, or VC, firm. These VC firms are basically pools

When presenting to a VC firm, go in overprepared. Pull out all the stops with that market research you just completed to prove that your business is bringing to market a unique and desirable product. Make sure your business plan is detailed and fact-supported or you won't last five minutes before the firm rejects your proposal.

of money from high-wealth individuals who are looking to get a high rate of return on their investments. They are willing to take much greater risks than banks, but they also set a much higher interest rate for loans and often take a piece of the business. It is painful to give up equity at this early stage, but it can be worth it if the alternative is no funding at all.

There are many VC firms to choose from, and each one usually specializes in a single industry or business type. They are experts in evaluating business ideas and risk against existing market conditions, competition, and manufacturing alternatives, among other factors. To find the right VC fund for your business, attend local chamber of commerce or other business group meetings and start networking. Find out who in your area might specialize in your industry and has a good reputation. That banker who turned you down for your loan might still be able to help you by referring you to a VC firm with a good reputation. Each firm operates differently, so investigate several before selecting which one you want to do business with.

Crowdfunding

It can be extremely difficult for a small business or an individual inventor to get funding through traditional pathways when he or she has little collateral to offer and no sales track. Fortunately, over the past few years a new type of fund-raising system, called crowdfunding, takes advantage of Internet-based social networks and has gained in popularity. Crowdfunding is like friends' loans on steroids; it gathers money from a lot more people than just your friends. There are basically two types—donation-based and equity-based—as well as some hybrids that combine these models.

DONATION-BASED CROWDFUNDING

The donation-based model of crowdfunding is an online fund-raising strategy that seeks donations from large pools of individuals, stretching well beyond any one inventor or entrepreneur's immediate circle, in exchange for rewards or, increasingly, with pre-orders if the donation is funding the production of a consumer good. Rock bands have financed albums and tours through crowdfunding; teachers have funded classrooms; nonprofits have matched grants. Countless organizations from every sector of the economy have sought and received support for their projects this way.

There are many donation-based crowdfunding sites—for example, Quirky and RocketHub—each catering to a specific demographic and type of industry. At the time of this writing, by far the two most popular such sites are Kickstarter and Indiegogo.

KICKSTARTER Known for hosting the most highly funded campaigns to date, Kickstarter was launched in 2009, and since then, donors have pledged more than $450 million to the projects of their choice (the average campaign runs about $5,000). Projects are highly selective and limited to a specific number of categories, generally involving entertainment, the arts, and technology. Increasingly, however, Kickstarter is becoming known as a place where entrepreneurs can find backing for new, cool consumer products.

Here's how it works: An inventor creates a page for his product, essentially pitching it to explain why it's a worthwhile investment and why it's important. Then he sets a funding goal and deadline. If people get excited about the product and want to see it succeed, they can pledge money, essentially pre-ordering the product. There is usually an incentive attached to each level of pledge—for example, your name on the company website for $100; a first edition of the product and your name on the company website for $150; a year's supply of the product, two tickets to the launch party, and your name on the company website for $200, and so on and so forth. If the project reaches its funding goal by the deadline, the donors' credit cards are charged, they receive whatever reward accompanied their pledge, and Kickstarter receives a 5 percent fee. If the project falls short, no one is charged and the inventor receives no money. Funding on Kickstarter is all-or-nothing. Project initiators retain all control over their product and business.

Two of my *Shark Tank* entrepreneurs, Kelley Coughlan and Jenn Deese, are the inventors of the Pursecase, a phone case designed to look like a tiny purse for the woman who wants to go out carrying only the essentials. It protects your phone, but also holds credit cards, cash, and ID. They successfully raised enough money to fund their first product run on Kickstarter, though the process was not as seamless as they would have hoped.

First, they researched other successfully funded Kickstarter projects to see what those entrepreneurs did right, and ascertained what financial goal they thought they could reasonably attain. They created a polished video, did a photo shoot of their product, and wrote compelling marketing copy. At the time of their launch, in early 2013, Kickstarter's success stories were receiving a significant amount of coverage from online media outlets like TechCrunch and Mashable, and Coughlan and Deese hoped to reap the benefits of the heightened awareness.

Beginning with a heavy social media campaign to their friends and family networks, the pair quickly raised about $3,000 in the first week. Then donations stalled. Coughlan and Deese now say, "We were prepared for [a stall], but we weren't prepared for how long that stall would last." No matter how hard they worked to expand their donor base and get media attention for their project, donations remained at a trickle, and in fits and starts. The Kickstarter audience just wasn't responding to Pursecase's product.

That's when Coughlan and Deese realized something. As might have been surmised by the type of online media covering the Kickstarter story, which addressed primarily a tech and innovation audience, the Kickstarter donor population was heavily male. It was the women in the audience who liked their idea; there just weren't enough of them on the site.

One welcome Kickstarter connection they did make, however, was a manufacturer who found them through the site and offered to make their purses for less than their current manufacturer. Realizing that they would never meet their fund-raising goal in time, but reassured by the fact that now they no longer needed as much of a down payment to get their product made, they decided to go with plan B.

When a fund-raising project stalls, donors get discouraged and generally opt to save their money for something that has a better chance of succeeding. To keep the project moving forward and encourage further donations, the inventionistas asked a generous friend to loan them money in the form of donations made in small increments over time, so the pledge total would continue to increase. This encouraged further giving. Ultimately, the pair earned only $13,000 of their $35,000 target and had to infuse the project with their own cash to meet their goals and keep the money they had actually raised. They immediately returned the money they owed the benefactor who kept the project going, and in the end they did earn enough cash to pay for their first round of inventory. Though the ride was a little bumpy, Coughlan and Deese have no regrets. Not only did they raise the money necessary to launch their company but they also made connections through Kickstarter that have proved invaluable to their business, including their current equity partner.

Coughlan and Deese's story is a classic example of how inventors have to be prepared for anything, and turn every situation, no matter the outcome, into a learning experience that will ultimately benefit their business. And the Pursecase is a great seller to date!

INDIEGOGO Similar to Kickstarter except that it does not curate projects, Indiegogo's level of innovation represented is generally somewhat lower, but there is a broader range of products and business for donors to choose from. In addition, charities and even individuals can raise money on the site for any cause, such as the campaign to send a bullied bus monitor in New York State on a well-deserved vacation (which raised over $700,000). Though the cachet of some projects may sometimes be a little lower, Indiegogo's advantage over Kickstarter is that it only charges a 4 percent fee for successful projects; for a 9 percent fee, it allows you to keep whatever funds you raise even if you fail to meet your projected goal. Indiegogo projects only have about a 20 percent success rate, however, compared to Kickstarter's 44 percent.

GOFUNDME A crowdfunding site for just about everything, Go-FundMe is for just about anyone, so long as he or she has a Facebook page. GoFundMe taps your social networks for money. People have raised money to pay for surprise birthday parties, medical bills, and surgery to heal an abused puppy's broken hips. GoFundMe receives a 5 percent fee per donation, and the donations are paid out as they come in. Recently the site launched an all-or-nothing reward-based campaign option, like those on Kickstarter, which is specifically targeted to help fund the individual projects of artists, inventors, and entrepreneurs.

IN SUM, THERE ARE A NUMBER of pros and cons to crowdfunding:

PROS
- You can test the market and gauge demand for your product.
- It allows you to raise capital without giving away equity.
- You can mobilize an audience that will become loyal fans, eager to see you succeed. (Kickstarter donors became Coughlan and Deese's biggest supporters and actively promoted their product on social media platforms.)

CONS
- If your product appeals to a different target demographic than that of the crowdfunding

platform, your market testing will be flawed and
getting backers will become much more difficult.

- The amount of time you put into your campaign
directly correlates with how much money you raise;
attracting backers is basically a full-time job.
- On Kickstarter, if you don't raise the full amount you
ask for, you don't get any money at all.
- If you haven't taken the correct steps to protect your
idea through a patent or trademark before running
your campaign, you're at high risk for idea theft.
Factories looking for ideas and new products
regularly trawl crowdfunding sites for ideas they can
steal and quickly knock off.
- Crowdfunding campaigns run online forever; failure
to complete a campaign will always be "Googleable"
and may damage your reputation.
- The crowdfunding market has become saturated,
especially on Kickstarter, and so it has grown more
difficult to break through the clutter; some donors
may be experiencing burnout.

EQUITY-BASED AND HYBRID CROWDFUNDING

A relatively new form of crowdfunding, equity-based models
started gaining momentum following the passing of the Jump-
start Our Business Startups (JOBS) Act of 2012, which was a
bipartisan law aimed at reducing the extent of securities regulations so that private companies could solicit investments from
the public. Crowdfunding sites that offer equity, like CircleUp
and AngelList, give investors a stake in the outcome of the project or company they decide to finance. Whereas the donations

Have a backup plan. Not all crowdfunding projects meet the required goal.

on sites like Kickstarter come in small but steady streams, the money exchanged on equity sites can range from the thousands of dollars to the tens of thousands of dollars.

In addition to strictly equity-type crowdfunding sites, there are hybrids like the popular Crowdfunder, which offers a blend of donation-based and investment crowdfunding. Similarly, Fundable is like Kickstarter in that inventors and entrepreneurs can solicit reward-based donations to fund their business, but it also offers new start-ups the option of choosing to raise their capital through several crowdfunding strategies, including equity- and debt-based donations. In addition, Fundable brings together distribution companies, retailers, and other brands looking for the next new thing. As of this writing, it charges $99.00 per month to fund-raise. As in all crowdfunding, inventors should proceed with caution.

THE RANGE OF CROWDFUNDING OPTIONS can be a bit mind-boggling, especially when each site caters to various small-business needs. Plus, crowdfunding sites constantly make changes to how they do business, and they rise and fall in popularity, so always do your research and make sure to stay abreast of whatever new options become available. Magazines like *Entrepreneur* or *Inc.* often write articles or publish lists related to crowdfunding sites that can help you determine which one is right for you.

Creative Funding Sources

If you've exhausted all traditional fund-raising channels, or you want to make sure you've left no stone unturned in the hunt for capital, get creative. It's like what you do when you're hunting for your misplaced car keys—when you've looked in all the usual places, start looking in the unusual ones.

GOVERNMENT GRANTS

The advantage of grants is that they do not need to be repaid. However, they are not free, in that getting them takes a heck of a lot of work. Competition for grants is high, the grant-writing process can be extremely complicated, the various grant sources often have stringent reporting standards, and there are usually strict limits on how you are allowed to use the funds. Grants aren't appropriate for every business, either. For example, federal grant money cannot be used to launch new businesses, and most small businesses do not qualify for federal grants. For that, you generally need to turn to state or local entities.

> **If you accept a grant, be sure you understand what percentage of your business, or portion of your product revenue, you will owe the government.**

Grants are useful, however, if you have already launched your business and want to use them to fund additional research and product development, especially in science, agriculture, or technology. Grants are usually awarded with the understanding that they will be used in conjunction with matching funds or a loan.

DRTV COMPANIES

Direct response television (DRTV) companies are different from television shopping channels like HSN or QVC. The DRTV companies sell products on television through short-form spots—one or two minutes—or long-form infomercials, which last thirty minutes (we'll call them both infomercials here). QVC's programming is a form of direct response television, but QVC is a home shopping channel, not a DRTV company. One of the differences is that on a home shopping channel, a presenter may offer any number of products for sale in a segment, whereas an infomercial is typically dedicated to a single product. A home shopping channel also works hard to build a long-term relationship with its viewers.

While some DRTV companies promote their own products, like Ronco, others typically promote products licensed from others. In fact, they will even fund new products. There is often a catch, though. While DRTV companies may seem like attractive partners, some can also be a little like the Sirens of Greek mythology, luring you closer with beautiful songs until you dash yourself on the rocks. If a legitimate DRTV company truly wants to support your business idea, it should also be willing to put up the money to produce and test-market the infomercial.

Many companies will tell you that they love, love, love your idea, but

Also, negotiate a quick exit in your contract. Give the company a short bracket of time in which to decide whether or not to move forward with your product, and if the infomercial doesn't work, make sure you get 100 percent of your product rights back in no longer than 60 days after the test.

beware if they want you to put up the money to film the info-mercial and pay for the media time (the air time for running it on TV). It is expensive, and paying for it yourself is extremely risky because the infomercial success rate is exceedingly low. I generally wouldn't recommend that you fund the production and media testing of your own infomercial. If a DRTV company is interested in making an infomercial for your product, they should be willing to pay for the production, make molds if needed, source and finance your inventory, and pay for the media time.

Typical royalty rates in deals in which the DRTV company assumes all responsibilities and risks range between 1 and 3 percent of gross revenues. If you have a patent, you may be able to get a slightly higher rate. One additional note of caution: some contracts give the DRTV company exclusive rights to your product for years, making it impossible for you to take it anywhere else. Be extremely careful what you sign, and if at all possible have an attorney review the contract to be sure you are not being asked to give up too much. Try to insist on some form of performance benchmark (like a minimum annual royalty) in order for the DRTV company to retain its rights to your product. Your attorney may have other suggestions to protect your interests, and it is usually worth spending the money to get advice on how to ask for what you want in language

Be leery if a DRTV company is salivating over your product, even though every other expert and lender has shown extreme caution and has backed away.

that is most likely to elicit a favorable response. At the very least, make sure that before signing any agreement you understand exactly what rights you are granting, what rights you retain, and for how long the contract will remain in effect.

CONTESTS

Kevin O'Leary has compared *Shark Tank* to a bank. He calls it the "Bank of Tank," as a matter of fact. And indeed, *Shark Tank* and contests like it are marvelous opportunities in today's tough economic climate, providing many inventors with much-needed capital even as banks turn people down when they would have easily qualified for loans just a few years ago. The more popular *Shark Tank* gets, the more local businesses, chambers of commerce, and even mayor's offices are sponsoring similar product and business idea contests, though on a smaller scale.

Typically, the winner gets a cash prize and mentoring from local business people, who can give an inventor access to machine shops, marketing experts, and other resources that can help them steer their idea to the next level of production and sales. The influx of capital might not be as large as what a successful contestant might get through a deal on *Shark Tank*, but it's something (without any obligation to give up equity), and the access to expertise can be invaluable.

If you enter a contest, enter to win. You cannot overprepare. Familiarize yourself with the criteria for the contest and tailor your pitch to match. As you pitch, address the judges by name; though your presentation should be well rounded, find ways to link your product or idea with each judge's specialties or interests. Be ready to answer any question. The top ones will be:

- What's your market?
- What will your product cost and what can you sell it for based on the competition?
- Is your product patent-protectable?

Make sure you know the results of your market research cold. Ideally, solicit manufacturing quotes ahead of time so that all of your production numbers are fact-based, not best guesses. Kevin O'Leary says he has reviewed the tape of every deal in which an entrepreneur got funded and found that, "One hundred percent were able to articulate the opportunity in 90 seconds or less, showing me why if I were an investor I would make money. That's crystal clear in every case."

YOUR FAMILY REVISITED

If your loved ones are living in fear while you're out there living your dream, you're all going to have a miserable experience, even if you do eventually succeed. What's the point of achieving your dream if you lose everything else that really matters in the process? As you negotiate ways to raise capital, if you have a family, or share your life with a partner, keep in mind that your journey is their journey, too. Even if they know everything you're doing is to secure their future and maybe even build something to pass on to future generations, it can be scary to family members to watch you put yourself on the line, especially when their lives are going to be affected by the decisions you're about to make.

It's crucial that you keep your parent, spouse, or partner informed, and if at all possible, involved, too. Do not quit your day job before discussing the consequences and implications that decision will have with your family. Do not secretly take out a second mortgage on your house. Having open and honest discussions will be crucial to building the trust and support you'll need from your spouse or partner as you move forward.

As discussed in Chapter 1, discussing worst-case scenarios is important to establishing confidence and trust. A critical part of your conversations must include the following question: What's the worst thing that could happen? Then you have to ask: Can we deal with the consequences? Discuss worst-case scenarios and establish how you will handle them. You'll both feel better if you're on the same page and prepared for any eventuality. Do not shy away from these difficult conversations.

The start-up inventor's road is an extremely hard one. Don't take it alone if you don't have to. Whenever possible, enlist your family in your business. That doesn't mean you should necessarily work side by side every day—you know best how much togetherness your relationships can handle!—but do whatever you can to make them feel like they are a part of your new endeavor. It will keep you close with a common goal and a common bond. If you keep your family involved, you'll encounter a lot less resentment from whoever has to pick up the slack, or spend more time alone, while you are holing up in your office until 3 a.m., or traveling to meet buyers, or inspecting your factory. And they will willingly put in the hours to help you—for free—especially when they understand that, ultimately, everything you're doing is for them.

It's easy for inventors and budding entrepreneurs to be so excited about a dream that they underestimate the impact their pursuit of those dreams will have on their partner or family, or they dismiss their concerns. Believing in an inventor's dream is one thing. Committing to an enormous financial risk that could have long-term implications to your future and that of your family is quite another. If your partner questions the wisdom of accepting a loan or the terms of an investment, do not accuse the individual of being unsupportive. Make sure to explain how you intend to use the money, and how you intend to make it back. Don't make promises and expect your partner to take you at your word. Show the person a well-thought-out financial plan and be prepared to answer any questions patiently and respectfully.

Dan was supportive of my efforts from the very beginning. If I believed my product was a hero, so did he. He didn't argue when I told him I wanted to make my earring organizer and jump into it full time (at the time I was writing plays and reading scripts at Chicago's Victory Gardens Theater). He didn't try to talk me out of using our savings account to fund my design drawings, prototypes, and the travel expenses I would incur to pitch to retailers around the country. I only felt comfortable taking out the loan I would need to pay the $120,000 manufacturing quote after my market research confirmed that about 90 percent of the women who saw my earring organizer said they would buy it.

Dan and I had a long talk. I outlined to him the cost of the tools I'd need to make the organizer, as well as all the other expenses I had calculated so far, and I shared with him how I intended to pay back the loan. He told me to go for it. Among the many things we have in common, one of them is that we stand behind our beliefs. I was certain my invention was going to sell, and that was enough for him. He knew I could do it. And with his trust and emotional support, I knew I could do it, too. Ultimately, I collateralized the loan with our home, but I reached out to a group of other family members and put a plan in place in case the earring organizer failed. If that happened, they would help me pay down the loan until I got back on my feet, ensuring that Dan and I wouldn't lose our home. As I've shared, I was confident I wouldn't have to put that plan into effect, though. Everything was telling me that my invention was going to be a hit. Now I just had to make it and sell it.

FUNDING TO-DO LIST:

❑ Write a business plan.

❑ Calculate your business valuation.

❑ Investigate best funding sources.

❑ Develop a good presentation.

❑ Secure family support.

6

THE TRUTH ABOUT PATENTS

"One idea can change your future."
—AUTHOR UNKNOWN

ONE OF THE FIRST THINGS I DID AFTER DESIGNING MY FIRST INvention was to file for a patent, and I now hold over 120 of them. That should tell you something about how important and valuable I believe they are. Yet many inventors don't file for patents. There are several legitimate reasons why they make this decision, the primary one being cost. Often, too, an idea is not patentable.

Many inventors have gone on to enjoy success without patents, so it's certainly not a necessity. Yet a patent arms you with so much more leverage should you have to defend your idea in court and in the marketplace. So if it is remotely within the range of possibility, I would urge you to try to get one. While the preparation of the application and its prosecution before the patent office won't ever be free, it does not have to be prohibitively expensive, either. That said, ultimately it's an extremely personal choice. Some people can't move forward confidently without one; others believe forgoing a patent is a manageable risk. So while this chapter explores the reasons why a patent is worthwhile, and the various ways entrepreneurs can go about getting one, at the end of this chapter I'll discuss your strategic options should you choose not to file for a patent.

THE THREE BENEFITS OF PATENTS

1. Patents = Protection

Patents are your best protection against copycats. The United States operates under a first-to-file patent system. Until just a short while ago, we operated under a first-to-invent system. So, let me explain the difference. Say I invented a product, going so far as to create a working model, but I didn't file for a patent. Under the first-to-invent system, if you came along after me and filed a patent for an invention extremely similar to mine, I could start something called an "interference proceeding" and claim rights to the invention, so long as I could prove that I had invented the idea first. Unfortunately, under this system inventors constantly found themselves in court fighting for the rights to their own inventions, an extremely costly process.

The old system was also a problem for the other guy. Many people ceased developing their ideas because they didn't feel they could adequately protect them. There was no way to know whether the minute you filed for a patent someone wouldn't pop up out of the woodwork and claim that he had thought of the idea first. And then you were out of luck, because the law was on the side of the person who thought of the idea first, not the person who filed the patent first.

To solve this problem, in 2011, Congress introduced a bill called the America Invents Act, which switched the United States from a first-to-invent system to one followed by most other countries in the world, a first-to-file system. In fact, I was honored that the U.S. Patent and Trademark Office (USPTO) interviewed me at the time so that I could explain how such a bill would affect small businesses. I got to attend the signing of the bill and even had President Obama sign my first patent. I believe this new system is fairer and more straightforward.

Under this new system, however, the burden is on *you* to file for a patent as soon as possible, or risk getting scooped. By avoiding the cost of filing for a patent for your new invention, you could potentially lose all the money you think you're saving—and more, in the future, if someone steals your idea and simply files a patent for it ahead of you. That person could even come after you for patent infringement, and you could lose all rights to your invention.

We live in a world that thrives on knockoffs. It's incredible how many individuals and companies make their fortunes copying other people's ideas and products. They're out there, looking for easy marks, certain that you won't have the money, the backing, or the backbone to fight them if they steal from you. Sometimes, if your product has great promise, a company that wants to sell it will take up the lawsuit for you, but that's a long shot. So with or without a patent, you are in for the fight of your life. But without a patent, you're reduced to fighting with bare fists; a patent arms you with weapons and a shield.

If you have a patent and someone infringes upon it, you have options. Your attorney can send your competitor a cease-and-desist letter, giving the person the chance to willingly take his product off the market. (If that doesn't work, you can alert your competitor's retailers to the fact that they are buying from a seller who is willfully infringing on a patent.) Retailers really don't like to deal with products that are involved in patent litigation. However, this can go both ways, so get advice from an attorney first. Without a patent, there wouldn't be much you could do about someone's stealing your idea and selling your product. A patent puts the law on your side and gives you the leverage that you otherwise do not have.

TWO IMPORTANT THINGS TO REMEMBER:

1. The biggest mistake you can make is failing to learn from your mistakes, because that means you'll commit those mistakes again.

2. The harder the battle, the stronger and smarter you'll be at the end, no matter the outcome.

2. Conduct Due Diligence

It would be a tragedy to put your heart and soul, not to mention perhaps your life savings, into an idea only to find out once you try to start selling it that there is already something else exactly like that on the market. Now, if you're like every other inventor I've ever met, you probably think this is highly unlikely. You believe without a doubt in the uniqueness of your product. And you may be right. Or you may be like those seven women I met when I was consulting for Oprah's Next Big Thing event in Los Angeles, all unknowingly pitching the same diaper bag.

You're already traveling a rough road; the fewer surprises you have to face, the better. You have probably already done some research yourself. The minute that idea popped into your head, you probably sat down at your computer to see if you could find anything out there that resembled it. I hope you left no online stone unturned, trawling all the Internet vendors, search engines, and social networks, like Pinterest, Bing, Google, Facebook, Tumblr, Twitter, Flickr, and Instagram. You also should have looked at every retailer's website that could conceivably carry your product, from the online shopping networks like QVC and HSN, to the large merchandisers' websites like Amazon, Walmart, Target, and Bed Bath & Beyond; from the big general department stores like Nordstrom, Macy's, JCPenney, and Bloomingdale's, to the specialty retailers that cater exclusively to your market. This might mean Home Depot if you've invented a tool, or Academy if you've invented a new type of fishing rod, but it could also be the independent, high-end maternity and baby store in your area if you've invented, say, a diaper bag.

And of course while you've been out walking around, you've probably been keeping your eyes peeled. The thing is, just because you're not finding a product like yours on the Web or on retail shelves, that doesn't mean a competitor doesn't exist, or even that no one will challenge you when you try to sell your product. If you start selling an item, and someone has a patent on it, you may be guilty of patent infringement. Your competitor would be within his rights to try to shut you down with a cease-and-desist order, or force you to pay a royalty should you continue to sell.

It's smart to be well aware of the market so that you don't set yourself up for problems. One good resource could be the patent application process, in which the first step is to mine the USPTO database for any information that could preclude you from getting a patent. If you have no funds and no way to budget for an attorney, you can do this search yourself. But if you can, it is better to hire an expert. Patents are notoriously difficult to read and understand—the legalese can be almost unintelligible.

Patent attorneys, also known as intellectual property attorneys, go to school for many years to learn how to read and write them. These lawyers will simply know more than you possibly could about all the rules and subtleties within patent law. Their search will necessarily be more exhaustive than one that you could conduct on your own. Like you, they will search the USPTO website, and may search other online search engines. Unlike you, they will have a thorough understanding of the patent classification system and actually know what they are doing. They have years of experience that a beginner entrepreneur just won't have. While you may not think something is similar or could prohibit you from getting a patent, they might know otherwise.

If you visit the USPTO website, you'll find that, at first, the process doesn't seem so daunting. The site even provides you with a seven-step guide to help you conduct your search. But although brainstorming keywords and investigating the class and subclasses in which your product could be categorized may not sound hard, if you're doing it correctly and thoroughly, it will probably be a painfully slow process. And how will you know that you have thought of *every* keyword that could possibly relate to your product? What if it could be categorized under a certain subclass that you didn't think to check? Your attorney can make sure that no details slip through the cracks, details that could come back to haunt you later.

The attorney will do two different types of searches: (1) A patentability search to check to see if there are already other patents (or "prior art") in existence that could prevent you from getting your patent; and (2) an infringement search, which checks to make sure that by selling your product you are not inadvertently infringing on someone else's patent. Though this step is not routinely done, I think it's a smart thing to do and I recommend it. This comprehensive search alone can be worth the price of your attorney.

Based on the results of these searches, your lawyer will be able to tell you the likelihood that you will get your patent. If your attorney believes that you have a good shot, you can decide whether it's worthwhile to continue. And if your attorney is doubtful you'll get your patent, you can stop trying to get one. Either way, now you have done due diligence and possess important information about the competitive landscape, which will allow you to make an educated decision about the best way to proceed.

3. Investors Love Patents

A patent makes your product more appealing to investors because it reassures them of your ability to corner the market, which gives them a better chance of profiting from their investment. It also gives them something to sell if, for any reason, their investment in you doesn't pan out. Even if they love your idea, they don't really need you—they need your patent. You will have a much easier time getting funding and finding partners if you can claim that you hold a patent on your invention.

THE COST FOR FILING FOR A PATENT

Filing for a patent may cost you less than you think. Your initial layout for an intellectual property lawyer could be anywhere from $2,500 to $15,000, depending on the type of patent you are pursuing, the seniority of your attorney, what firm you use, and what city you live in. For example, if you are filing for a patent for a simple product, it might be less expensive than if you were filing for something in biotech, which is much more involved and costly.

There are steps you can take to minimize the cost of filing:

- A relatively inexpensive junior attorney will still know a lot more than you do and would be well worth the investment.

- There are ways you can minimize your fees, too. A basic filing fee for a utility patent currently costs $1,600, but if you qualify as a small entity, which means you employ fewer than 500 employees, that cost is reduced by half. And as a result of the America Invents Act, as of spring 2013, you can also apply as a micro-entity if you qualify, in which case your fee would drop by 75 percent to $400. Filing for a provisional patent could cost an inventor as little as $65. Filing for a patent does not have to be an exorbitant investment, especially if you can figure out a way to mitigate the cost of a patent attorney.

- You can file your patent yourself online. It's called filing "pro se," and it costs about a thousand dollars. It's not easy—a patent is rarely granted after the initial filing and almost always requires some back-and-forth between the applicant and the patent examiners who believe they have found reason to reject a claim—but it can be done.

> The USPTO online State Resources page offers lists of registered patent attorneys, resource centers, law clinics, inventor organizations, and pro bono services available in each state. Go to uspto.gov/inventors/state-resources.

WHILE I STRONGLY BELIEVE that it is a worthwhile investment to spend the money on someone who can help you put your best foot forward, who knows the ins and outs of patent law and can increase the likelihood that you will get your patent, the last option sometimes works. I knew an inventor with a clever idea who filed for her patent for herself, and she got it. We wound up working together and her product sold well. For certain products, especially simple ones, it may be worth a shot if the alternative is not to file at all.

FIVE STEPS TO OBTAINING A PATENT

1. Hire a Patent Attorney

As I said, I advise inventors to file for their own patents only as a last option. If you wouldn't feel qualified to go into court and fight your own case, you shouldn't try to file your own patent, if you can help it. A patent application has to be written with extreme caution—every word matters. Attorneys understand the system, they know the pitfalls, and they are worth the investment. In addition, filing your own patent actually lowers your chance of getting the patent, because you just don't know what you don't know. Some researchers estimate that the number of inventors who fail to obtain patents after filing pro se may be as high as 75 percent.

Not every lawyer is qualified to handle patent law, which is exceedingly complex and nuanced. Before hiring your intellectual property attorney, ask around, do your research, get recommendations. There are two things you want to find out at this stage:

1. Does this attorney specialize in an area relevant to your product? All registered patent practitioners have a technical degree, such as chemical, mechanical, or electrical; you want an attorney who knows your field as well, if not better, than you do.

2. Is the attorney a patent prosecutor or a litigator? Unlike the prosecutors you've seen on television, patent prosecutors don't actually try anyone in court. Rather, they are the attorneys who write the patents and submit them to the USPTO in Washington, D.C. A patent litigator, on the other hand, fights patent infringement cases.

Before hiring a patent attorney, make appointments with your candidates and meet with them in their offices. This is extremely important, and not just because you're about to spend some money. As in every profession, there are good attorneys, great attorneys, and attorneys you need to avoid like the plague. It's always going to be a mixed bag. You've got to meet your potential candidates in person and question them about your product. Do they seem to understand your field and the technology behind your idea? Do they seem confident that they would know how to prosecute a patent for a product like yours? The person you hire to file your patent will be taking your future into his or her hands. It's crucial that you like and trust your attorney and that you feel confident he or she will successfully get you a patent.

It is possible that you could go through all the trouble and expense of filing a patent, and still be denied. Only an experienced, dogged patent attorney will, it is hoped, be able to help you get around that roadblock. You also want to hire someone who will be honest with you about the likelihood of your getting your patent, so that you don't waste your money. But if all goes well and you bring more products to market in the future, this could be the beginning of a long relationship. You want to feel good about this partnership.

After your attorney conducts a patentability search and believes that your idea is eligible for a patent, you will begin the filing process. Remember, a search is not necessary, but I recommend it because it helps your attorney draft a better patent.

2. Choose Your Patent

Individual inventors generally pursue three types of patents. The most common are utility and design, though there is a third, plant patents, for the agricultural arena. A *utility* patent protects the function of a product or idea, the actual mechanics of how it works. A *design* patent, on the other hand, protects the aesthetic of the product. The only thing a patent examiner will look at upon receiving a request for a design patent is its similarity to existing designs. A design patent is easy to get, but also harder to defend because sometimes it is easy for a competitor to work around it by making a few small changes.

> Your money will be better spent filing for a utility patent, because even though it is harder to get, it is easier to defend. If at all possible, file for the stronger protection of a utility patent. Often, however, you can get both kinds of patents.

Some people first file a provisional patent application. Inventors often do this when they haven't quite cemented the details of their invention. It's a stopgap, an inexpensive way to get your filing date on the books, so you can protect your idea per the rules of the first-to-file system, while giving you a chance to make sure the product is good and that there is a market for it before bothering with the additional expense of a utility patent. Your provisional patent application will outline all the important details about your invention. If you filed a provisional patent application, you have one year in which to file for your utility patent; otherwise the provisional expires and you lose the benefit of an earlier date.

3. Write Your Claims

Once you've decided which type of patent you are going to file, your patent attorney will file a number of claims. The first is your *independent claim*, which includes all the main, minimum elements you want to cover. You will want your main claim to be as broad in scope as possible. You will then have *dependent claims* in addition to the main claim that further narrow the scope of protection.

In my first patent on my earring organizer, my broad, independent claim called for a "base having a plurality of grooves and a plurality of separate stands, each being received in a groove." One of my dependent claims added the fact that "each stand had a crosspiece extending between respective supports of the stands." (Now you understand, from reading that language, why people shouldn't attempt this without an attorney.) Notice that I wasn't specific about the height, length, or the material used. You always want to draft your claims as broadly as possible so as not to limit the scope for things like size or materials, which would narrow your protection. It is important to have claims of varying scope to well protect your invention from challenges of invalidity, which a defendant in a patent infringement lawsuit will often claim.

Once your patent is filed with the USPTO, it gets stamped and dated. And then you wait, because at any given time, there is usually a backlog of about 600,000 patent applications ahead of you at the USTPO, waiting to be processed. At this stage, your product is *patent pending*. Some people choose to wait before moving forward, but most people continue to pitch their idea to buyers and make, market, and sell it while they wait for their patent to be approved. I understand the instinct to be cautious, but it's better to get out there and sell because, for all you know, you may never get your patent. It would be a shame to lose time that you could have been selling, waiting for something that may never come. Sell now with the anticipation that all will go well and you'll get your patent. If you don't, you can decide what to do then. You don't have to stop selling if you don't get one. A patent is like insurance—you may need it, but you hope you won't. Nevertheless, it's good to have if you can get it.

Being able to say that your product is patent pending is like sending a warning signal to knock-off artists. You're still vulnerable to predators, like a lamb in a field. But with a patent, or at least with the application of a patent on file, you're a lamb in a comfortable, safe enclosure. Without anything on record stating that you intend to defend yourself, you're a lamb who the wolves are watching. If an unscrupulous competitor or company spots your product and thinks they could make money with it, they'll look up your patent application and see if they can design around it. That's why it's important that you file good claims that are difficult to write around. Of course, if knock-off artists see that you haven't filed a patent at all, your invention is easy pickings, a tasty tidbit for a money-hungry wolf.

After you file, an examiner will start reviewing the USPTO database for "prior art." Prior art consists of any other patent (domestic or foreign), articles, books, catalogs, and even events that might tangentially have to do with your product. Keep in mind that you also have to tell the USPTO about any prior art you are aware of. The examiner digs for anything that could throw into question the originality of your idea and therefore make it undeserving of a patent. Most of the time, after this exhaustive search, the examiner will not send you a definitive yes or no; rather, you get something called an *office action*, a document that outlines which of your claims have been approved and elaborates on why others have been rejected. This is another reason why there's no point in waiting around biting your nails, praying for your patent to go through. It is rare for any patent application to sail through to approval intact on the first try.

4. Review Your Office Action

There are many reasons why you might not get a patent. One reason is that something too similar to your product already exists. There might not be much you can do about that. But another reason may be that your idea was judged to be too obvious. For example, though you may fervently believe that inserting an LED light into the brim of a baseball cap is wholly original, the examiner might determine that, in fact, adding a light to a cap is obvious—anyone could do it. Therefore, the invention does not warrant a patent. If this scenario were to happen—and it happens frequently—you would be glad you hired a patent prosecutor. On your own, it would be extremely hard to convince the examiner to reconsider. An experienced patent attorney, however, will be familiar with a host of previous legal decisions on which to base an argument that, in fact, your product is not obvious.

5. Decide Whether to Pursue Your Claims or Abandon the Application

As you review your office action, you and your attorney will discuss the results and decide whether to proceed in pursuing the patent. What's important to consider at this stage is not necessarily how many claims you think you can fight for, but *which* claims are worth fighting for. If the examiner's reply indicates that there is little prior art and your attorney is confident he or she can come up with a strong enough argument to turn around the rejection of an important claim, it's probably worth following through to get those claims, especially since you've already invested the money. If the only claims your attorney thinks he or she can get approved is a claim that doesn't offer you much protection because it's too narrow to be helpful, it's probably not worth the time and money to fight for it. And if your lawyer tells you that odds are you're never going to get your patent, why fight a losing battle? Stop, cut your losses, and continue to sell.

If you decide to pursue the patent, there can be a lot of back and forth as your attorney pushes back against disputed claims. There are usually several rounds during which the examiner denies some claims and grants others, and then your attorney responds with arguments as to why the claims should be granted. It's a process that can take a long time, depending on the arguments surrounding the patent.

A design patent can take as little as a year to obtain, but a utility patent can take longer. I had to wait almost seven years to get one of mine. Recently, however, the USPTO passed initiatives to help cut the time it takes to get a patent. You may have to pay a significant amount more to take advantage of the new programs, but it allows you to put your application on an accelerated track.

CONSIDER TRADEMARK PROTECTION, TOO

In addition to protecting your particular invention via patents, entrepreneurs should likewise consider securing trademark protection for their brands, logos, designs, and slogans. A trademark is any word or words, logos, slogans, or any combination thereof used as a source identifier for a product or service. In some circumstances, even the unique shape of a product can be protected as a trademark. It is important to understand that trademarks are not owned across all product and service categories and are limited only to the product category or categories for which a particular trademark is used. As such, the trademark CRC might be owned by one company in connection with lawnmowers, whereas the trademark CRC might also be owned by another company in connection with breakfast cereals. Since most lawnmower companies are not also in the business of breakfast cereals, consumers are unlikely to think that the parties' respective CRC products originate from the same source or company.

Generally speaking, trademarks can be earned in one of two ways in the United States. The first, common law or unregistered trademark rights, can be achieved merely by using a particular trademark in the marketplace in connection with a particular product or service. Common law trademarks are territorial and give one rights to the trademark in connection with a particular product or service only in the geographic region in which that person or business is using the mark. Conceivably, it is thus possible to have CRC branded lawnmowers for sale only in California. That will not cause any consumer confusion with another CRC branded lawnmower for sale by a different company only in New York since the geographic reach of these businesses does not overlap.

Second, trademark rights can be achieved by filing for federal trademark protection with the United States Patent and Trademark Office. Federal trademark rights are much broader than common law trademarks in that they are presumed to grant in the owner nationwide trademark rights and additional rights and remedies not available to common law trademark rights holders.

Obviously, it is critically important to protect one's brands as trademarks since some consumers rely on the brand for clues as to quality and reliability when making their purchasing decisions. Trademarks give the entrepreneur a monopoly power to be the sole user of a particular brand in connection with a particular product and service and the power to prevent a third-party copy-cat from using a confusingly similar name on a related product in the marketplace.

Much like preparing to patent your invention, it is critical to conduct your due diligence prior to using a trademark or logo in order to ensure it is available for use and protection. The first step is often to visit the United States Patent & Trademark Office (USPTO) website to make certain no third party owns a particular trademark in connection with a specific product or service. While you can certainly visit the USPTO website for some initial due diligence, you are likely best served by retaining a trademark attorney to conduct a complex full availability search so that you can appropriately assess availability of your new trademark and the likely risk associated, if any, with launching your new product or service under your new trademark. Once it is determined that your new trademark is a good candidate for your use and registration, your attorney will be able to prepare for you an application for registration of the trademark, in most cases for approximately $1,000 for a single class application.

HOW TO BRING YOUR PRODUCT TO MARKET WITHOUT A PATENT

Should you decide to abandon your patent application, or that you can't justify or shoulder the expense of applying for a patent in the first place, what then? Is it game over? No, because most products don't have patents or aren't patentable anyway. Just get it out there and try to blitz the market.

You will need to get your product onto the market first, and spread it to as many retailers as you can—the bigger the better—so that by the time a competitor gets its version out there, your product and brand have captured consumers' hearts and minds. Actually, you should plan to take this course of action even if you decide to file for a patent. It's always been my strategy to do both. Admittedly, for a new entrepreneur it's an uphill battle. It's not easy to get buyers to pay attention to you when you're unproven and unfamiliar. Like everyone else, they prefer to do business with known entities, and the major players have no incentive to take a chance on you. There are steps you can take to improve your chances, however.

- Hire a distributor or a firm with extensive retail connections to represent you (see Chapter 7 for more details on how these companies work).
- Get backing from a prominent investor to burnish your image.
- Appear on *Shark Tank* and make a deal with one of the shark investors to prove to buyers that the market wants what you've got—and the wave of free publicity won't hurt, either.

IN THE CASE OF *SHARK TANK*, THE sharks' expertise and clout can be extremely valuable. Even if you have to give away a percentage of your business, investors can help you get over the barriers to entry and get your product into many retailers so you can spread a wider net. And as everyone knows, once your foot is in the door, it's much harder for people to slam it in your face.

But imagine if you could do all of that with the additional protec-

The entrepreneur who puts in the most time, who is the most aggressive, who knocks on the most doors, who makes the best pitches, and who gets his or her product into the most retail locations wins.

tion of a patent? This wonderful, unique product you've invented probably means everything to you. A patent offers more than just protection; it gives you choices and the ability to determine your own fate. It's empowering, and that's priceless. Just ask the Drop Stop "Boyz." As they told me, "When the knockoffs and counterfeits started surfacing, it was like a blow to the guts. It hurt a lot. We felt helpless." It took them five years to finally get their patent so they could fight back. Today, almost all the copycats are out of business, and since we negotiated our deal on *Shark Tank*, the Drop Stop couldn't be doing better. They sold more product in three months after making our deal on *Shark Tank* than they did in three years on their own.

A surprising number of individuals receive patents and then never bring their product to market. Maybe something in their life changed and they lost interest in their invention. Maybe they only got the patent in case they decided they wanted to license the product one day. Maybe they just got tired of flying blind—it's only very recently that people have had easy access to information and programs that could educate them and show them examples of how other people did it. Or maybe they finally realized how hard it is to be an entrepreneur.

It takes a rare person to follow through with something like bringing an invention to market, and the patent process is just one of several difficult challenges you will face. But if you plan on being patient and persistent, and your market research is encouraging, and you're being creative and dogged in your pursuit of funds, and you're just overall prepared for the long haul, you're already way ahead of many of your peers and competitors.

PATENT TO-DO LIST:

1. Conduct due diligence to make sure there is no other product on the market like yours and to see if you could be infringing on someone else's patent. In order of importance, you should start with these online sites:

   USPTO database; Amazon; Google; online retailers; Facebook; Pinterest; general department stores; specialty retailers; Twitter; big box stores; Bing; Instagram; Flickr.

2. Hire a patent attorney, if at all possible.

3. If a patent attorney is out of the question, file pro se.

4. If forgoing a patent altogether, start blitzing the market.

5. Get a trademark, if applicable.

7

PITCH PERFECT

"Life is an echo. What you send out comes back."

—Zig Ziglar

SOMETIMES THE MOST INTERESTING *SHARK TANK* SCENES NEVER
make it on the air. In Season Four, three sharks (Daymond, Kevin,
and I) threw themselves into a bidding war for Aaron Krause's
happy yellow kitchen sponge, the Scrub Daddy. It was an exciting
episode. But left behind in the editing room was a moment when
Aaron thought his pitch almost went off the rails.

As Aaron told me later, when he learned that he would be
on *Shark Tank* he rehearsed his pitch for months. By then he
was learning to be a seasoned pitchman—he had recently made
it onto QVC and had pitched live on TV a couple of times. He
wanted to break into retail and get the Scrub Daddy nationwide.
Shark Tank was his big break, and he wasn't going to leave anything to chance. So he practiced, and practiced, and practiced,
preparing an answer for every question he thought the sharks
could possibly ask. Right before he walked out onto the set, he

found out that I would be in the tank. "One down, four to go," he thought, because he assumed that I would not be interested in doing a deal with him owing to his previous appearances on QVC. Then it was show time.

He pitched like a seasoned pro; he's a natural, like Billy Mays. He passed the sponge around so all the sharks could inspect it. His demonstration was seamless. Everything was going perfectly, and although he couldn't be sure, he felt confident he had our interest. Then, just as he finished reiterating the attributes that made the Scrub Daddy better than your average sponge—it doesn't scratch any surface, it scours off the toughest baked-on food, it turns hard in cold water and soft in hot water, and amazingly, it doesn't hold odors for several months—I took the product out of the package, wrinkled my nose, and asked, "What's that smell?" He was not prepared for that one, for he was sure the sponge didn't smell. His hopes sunk. He feared that he had just blown his chance of making a deal.

Thirty seconds into Aaron's pitch I knew I wanted to do a deal with him. But he didn't know that. And if his pitch hadn't been as dramatic, convincing, and pretty much perfect in every other way, it's possible that I might have questioned his credibility when I noticed an odd smell after he'd just assured us all that the Scrub Daddy never held odors. Fortunately, seconds later I recognized it as the smell of fresh ink from the new print on the box. That, coupled with the fact that Aaron was so professional, earnest, forthcoming, and funny—and that his product was so obviously a hero—made me confident that we would be great partners and we could make some serious money together. I offered him a deal, and after a bidding war with my fellow sharks, I won, and Aaron accepted.

Our partnership has paid off in a spectacular way, both professionally and personally. Within less than a year, we hit $15 million in retail sales, not only on QVC but also in Walmart, Bed Bath & Beyond, and many other major retailers across the country. Aaron's great, and the Scrub Daddy has fast become America's new favorite sponge. In addition, I treasure my new friendship with his whole family (his eight-year-old daughter texts me daily). And it all happened because Aaron's pitch was one of the strongest I'd ever seen—so strong that I instantly wanted his product.

> If you're prepared to pitch to a buyer, you're prepared to pitch to an investor, too. The only difference will be that an investor will press for more detailed information about your business's finances.

It is not possible to over-emphasize how incredibly important your pitch will be to the success of your product. In many cases, it will make or break your invention. If you've ever watched *Shark Tank*, you can tell that the entrepreneurs have rehearsed every gesture, every phrase, and every joke a million times; by the time they are presenting to us on the show, they could pitch their product walking backward. Even if you never present your product on national television, you should prepare for every pitch as though you were about to. The minute you walk into a buyer's office, you need to give the pitch of your life.

ANATOMY OF A PERFECT PITCH

It's Precise, Concise, and Enthusiastic

The first sentence out of your mouth should be as short as possible, yet also highlight your invention's top three selling features. For example, if I were pitching my fold-flat Christmas tree or my deluxe cosmetic box, I might say:

- This pre-lit five-foot fold-flat Christmas tree has 350 lights and folds completely flat so you can store it in less than three inches of space. To set up your tree, just twirl it open like a fan and secure with two twist ties, and voilà! Your decorating is done in three seconds flat.
- What does every woman need and wear? Makeup. This cosmetic organizer holds 100 pieces of makeup, all organized and in clear view, yet takes up only 9 x 6 inches of space on your counter. It swivels open so you can see all 100 pieces at a quick glance. Say goodbye to messy bins, clutter, and chaos in the morning.

Buyers are smart, savvy, and expert at summing up a product's potential at a quick glance. They don't need long-winded explanations (and if your product needs a long-winded explanation, you might rethink your product). Don't ramble or go off on tangents; it's boring and no buyer has time to listen. Be authoritative, clear, and excited! But also stay aware of your audience. If their body language says, "Go on," then go on. If it looks like you're losing them, switch to your product demonstration or wrap up and offer your buyers the opportunity to ask questions. Don't be so forceful that you turn them off. Be aware of people's moods and personalities and adjust as necessary. If they don't like or agree with something you say, think of another angle you could take that they might be more open to.

It's Exciting and Animated

Buyers listen to pitches all the time, and it's easy for one product presentation to blend into another if it's not exciting. So if you're lucky enough to get a buyer's few precious minutes, make those minutes memorable. Anytime you can make a buyer laugh or engage is a step closer to getting a deal. Help the buyer see that working with you could not only be a profitable experience but a fun one, too. Quality of life is key.

One of the most memorable pitches on *Shark Tank* that I ever experienced was also the craziest. It was for a weight-loss program—Lose 12 Inches in 12 Workouts—pitched by Ryan "Cowboy" Ehmann. He showed up in the tank wearing a bright cowboy shirt, big cowboy hat, chaps, and boots. Shortly into his pitch, he ripped open that cowboy shirt to show off his amazing abs. The only thing stronger than his superhuman abs was maybe his thick twang, which he used to excellent effect to keep us sharks engaged and asking questions.

I really like fun, energetic, zany people. Sometimes a little crazy is good. And Ryan definitely had that fun, zany energy going on. It's infectious, and laughter is a great selling tool. It makes you likeable. He was so wild and funny, literally screaming, "Yeehaw! Now, that's what I'm talking about!" He had my full attention. We were all really enjoying the pitch, and we couldn't stop watching. Ehmann was like a living embodiment of infomercial energy: his conviction and passion just pulled you in and made you want to watch. He was the biggest character I've ever encountered on *Shark Tank*.

Now, usually I'm hesitant about investing in weight-loss products, but I remember a woman on the Home Shopping Network several years earlier who had successfully sold a series of DVDs that taught people to lose weight by breathing differently. I was totally skeptical about her product, yet was amazed at how many she sold. It was unclear how her DVD worked, but she looked great and she was very convincing. She said that all you had to do was breathe in a certain way and you'd lose several pounds a week. Crazy, yes—but it sold! This woman made a fortune by tapping into people's desire to get results quickly and easily.

Ryan Ehmann reminded me of this woman in the way he could convince people that they could have amazing abs without a lot of effort. Breathing might have also been involved in his program. It was hard to understand how his product worked. I don't believe in enticing someone to think he or she can drop pounds without exercising or changing diet and I didn't feel the product was right for me, but Ehmann wound up making a deal with Daymond John for $125,000 and a 25 percent stake in his company. And he had one of the most memorable pitches owing to his zany enthusiasm. The last I heard, Daymond was promoting him as a pitchman, which would be perfect for him.

You don't have to walk into a room bare-chested to make a striking impression, and you don't need gimmicks. But do make sure that when you pitch, you exude confidence, drive, and dedication—so much, in fact, that you could pull a buyer out of a post-lunch stupor faster than any Red Bull. Often, when buyers or investors decide to do business with you, they're banking on you as much as they are banking on your product. So it's equally important for them to feel confidant that you're a good and reliable person to work with, and that you know what you are doing.

It Explains the Product's Appeal and Why Consumers Can't Live without It

I am big on enthusiasm. It's infectious. When you love your product, people see that, they wonder why you love it so much, and they start to like it, too. If I were eating a cracker and kept raving about the taste, you'd want to try it. Get your buyers as excited about your product as you are. Help them see the role it could play in their lives and that of others. Not everything will be right for the buyer personally, such as when you're selling a female-oriented product to a male buyer, but buyers know their customers. They get and understand them, and know what will be appealing, so male buyers can understand what women want, and vice versa.

It Answers Any Questions About Any Aspect of the Business, No Matter How Minute

You cannot overprepare for a pitch. Once you've got a good answer for every question a buyer could possibly throw at you, try to come up with two more. You need to know your business inside and out, and be able to explain yourself with authority. If you answer a question hesitantly, or you hem and haw, buyers and investors are going to wonder if you've really got everything under control and if you would be a reliable business partner. Remember, the buck stops with you.

You need to be accountable for and aware of every unit in the warehouse, every number on the books, every order coming in. In addition, you need to have ready answers for how you intend to plan for the future. And if you don't have an answer, don't lie; if you mess up, don't try to cover it up. Tell the truth. Say, "I'm not sure, I'll have to check on that," or, "I have that information and I'll get back to you." Don't try to act like you know everything if you don't. Never lie. People don't want to deal with someone they don't trust. And believe me, people can tell.

QUESTIONS ALMOST EVERY BUYER WILL ASK

What's the cost?

Where is it made?

How long will it take to make X amount of product?

Where else are you selling? What does it cost there?

Are there color choices?

What is the size and weight?

Is it patented?

Have you seen any competition?

What is your packaging like?

Can you drop-ship?

How many in a master carton?

If shipping from overseas, how many fit in a container?

Does it comply with all applicable laws and regulations?

If you are making claims about what your product can do,
   do you have third-party testing?

Your success will hinge not just on what you say but also on how you say it. For example, disagreeing with your buyers or investors isn't necessarily a kiss of death if you project the right attitude and can back your position up with solid facts and numbers. One of the most brutal *Shark Tank* pitches was the Marz Sprays pitch in Season Four. It was the last pitch of a long day and the air-conditioning wasn't working. All the sharks were tired, hot, and crabby. I had an important dinner to get to and I was already late. And in come a father-and-son team, the Marzes. They had what I thought was a great idea—vitamin sprays. They had a vitamin C spray, a sleep spray, a slim spray, and an energy spray. You didn't have to worry about swallowing pills or absorption; you just shot several sprays into your mouth and whichever spray you chose was immediately absorbed into your system.

I'm into vitamins and natural health, so I'm well educated and aware in these areas. I thought the idea was great; I chose to try the C-spray and really liked the product. My fellow sharks, however, being tired, chose the Reboot Energy Spray. Overzealously. Kevin, Daymond, Mark, and Robert each sprayed probably two to three times the recommended dose into their mouths, and within minutes became quite alert and rather voracious. Some of them started to fire questions dripping with skepticism. It wasn't

only that they didn't believe in the promise of the product—
everyone knows that, when swallowed, vitamins aren't easily absorbed into your intestinal tract. They were just suddenly much
more aggressive than they had been moments before. Obviously,
the Reboot spray really worked!

Though beads of perspiration dripped from their brows,
the Marz father and son held up under the pressure. They were
polite, they knew their answers, and under extremely rapid fire,
they bounced back. They were prepared and had great answers
for everything. It was memorable. They did a great pitch, and I
did a deal with them. I take the C-spray all the time, as does my
husband. Dan is like a cat with a fur ball when he tries to take a
pill, so these have been great for him and a relief to me.

It's Fact Based

When crafting your pitch, don't try to hype your product or idea,
or try to convince your buyer that your product is something it is
not. For example, one *Shark Tank* entrepreneur designed a clear
plastic water bottle with a rubberized, squeezable grip that allowed you to force the water through a carbon filter while you
drank. He worked tirelessly to convince us that his water bottle
was unique and that it represented a major improvement in water
bottle design. But it was just a filtered water bottle—a really expensive, fancy, filtered water bottle that didn't provide a much
bigger benefit than any other high-end water bottle could provide. In addition, he had little evidence to prove that consumers
were desperate to spend their money on his invention.

And unlike the Marz father and son, who knew their numbers, this inventor seemed to believe that if he just repeated over
and over again that his water bottle design was unique, we would
suddenly see the brilliance of his idea. He shouldn't have had to
work that hard. If your product is great, your market research is

accurate, and you present the features and benefits in a dynamic, convincing, and authoritative manner, your buyers or investors will be able to see for themselves that you're giving them the chance to be a part of something big and that you would make a great partner.

It Makes You Seem as Appealing as the Product

As you pitch, you should exude the positive energy of someone who is eager to work as a partner and a problem solver, someone who is take-charge and can make things happen. A buyer or investor is not always just investing in the product, but also in the person. Have you ever been on a job interview, and a potential boss asked you to tell him or her about your greatest weakness or your biggest mistake? The individual wasn't so interested in hearing about your failures as in hearing about how you handle challenges or how you might turn difficult situations around.

> You shouldn't have to convince any buyers that your product is a hero. If it's a hero, the facts should lead them to that inevitable conclusion.

While you don't want to highlight your mistakes or any struggles you've had with your business during a pitch, don't hide them, either. If your buyer asks you a question that can only be answered by admitting that you made a mistake, admit it. Be completely forthright and honest. Do not give buyers or investors any reason to think that you would hide something from them. There is always a way to present the challenges you've faced in a positive light.

One *Shark Tank* entrepreneur, Shelton, learned that lesson the hard way. She had designed a long, stretchy spaghetti-strap layering piece, a cross between a shell and an old-fashioned slip, that worked perfectly to help make many of today's short, sheer, and low-cut fashions easier to wear. She told her story and had some impressive sales. She had practiced her pitch and delivered it with energy and conviction. But there was one detail that didn't make any sense. She had sold a product similar to this one before and done well with it, then all of a sudden her sales had dried up, and she had stopped. Now she was back at it, with the same type of product, and I couldn't figure out why she'd had a two-year gap in sales.

I kept saying, "I don't understand; why did the sales stop for two years? Why did you end things with your partner when everything was going great?" Finally, when she realized her story really didn't make any sense, she broke down and admitted that during the time she was selling her first product, she had struggled with alcoholism. It ended her partnership, and she went into rehab. Hence the two years off and starting over. Her confession knocked the wind out of us. My heart went out to her because she seemed so distraught about having to share this information about her past. What she didn't realize was that she could have easily turned this part of her story into an asset.

> **Don't try to hide your business mistakes or failures, because you will eventually be found out. Be up front, explain how you overcame the obstacles in your path, and tell how you plan to make sure the situation doesn't repeat. Prove to buyers that you will be a trustworthy partner.**

An entrepreneur who has been to hell and back can only be wiser and stronger than her competitors. The fact that she had fought back from rock bottom actually made her story more compelling, and if she'd been up front with us about her circumstances, we wouldn't have thought twice about it, and we wouldn't have spent as much time circling around an issue that she clearly didn't want to discuss. She did not get a deal that day, but it was because none of us felt that her business was the right investment for us, not because of her past.

Buyers and investors are looking to work with entrepreneurs who are earnest, passionate, dedicated, and driven—all those qualities we covered in the first chapter of this book. Your pitch should allow you to emphasize all these characteristics. In addition, you will want to show buyers that you will be respectful and grateful for their time. It's no small thing for buyers to take a chance on a new inventor. Until you convince them otherwise, there's no reason for them to think that they need you. In fact, they know that even if they do decide to take a chance on you, you're going to be kind of a pain in the butt until you learn the ropes.

You'll get a booklet of information outlining all of the company's rules and regulations for fulfilling orders, but buyers know that you're bound to make mistakes and have questions. On top of that, your invention represents just one SKU, which is one product number. Buyers have to process a ton of new paperwork for every new vendor with whom they decide to do business. In addition, they have to teach new vendors all the rules for working within their organization. They often have to set up a new EDI (an electronic data interchange), so that their computers will recognize your product and be able to transmit information about it and to give and track orders. It costs thousands of dollars to set it up. They have to explain to you the proper way to ship, how to label, their rules, regulations, and requirements.

They're going to have to educate you, and they may not want to take the time or even have the time. Why bother with all that work for just one SKU when instead they could just continue to do business with the large corporations, the reps, or the distributors that represent a steady stream of new products from which to choose. Reps and distributors are helpful for the buyer and for you. As vendors they know the lay of the land and are already set up in the buyers' systems, which allows them to make transactions more seamless. It's not a bad choice for an entrepreneur to hire a rep to present their product. A rep's connections and broad reach can open doors that a lone inventor might not be able to on his or her own. Some stores even require that you use a distributor because they don't want to be bothered teaching individuals how to navigate their ordering system, and it's easier for them to work with just a few distributors who can supply them with a variety of merchandise.

Be aware that whenever buyers are watching your pitch, alongside all the excited thoughts of hugely successful quarters dancing in their heads are visions of the extra work you are going to make for them if they take a chance on you. So if you make the choice to go in without a distributor or a rep, convince your buyers you will be worth it. Be as helpful and handy as possible. Let them know not to worry, you'll take care of things, read their guidelines, and make sure you do everything right.

A FEW MORE SUGGESTIONS

Dress for Success

Not long ago, I read a surprising article that examined a trend in which people age fifty and over were beating twenty-somethings out of jobs because the twenty-somethings were showing up ill-dressed for their interviews, in sloppy or skimpy clothes. Our culture has many of us believing that manners and dress don't matter anymore. A lot of young people just out of college see social media titans and other hugely successful personalities show-ing up at stockholder meetings in a hoodie and jeans, and they think they can do the same when they pitch their product. After all, they're just keeping it real. But actually, they're not keeping it real, they're taking a real chance.

Once you're as successful as Mark Zuckerberg, then you can show up to important events dressed any way you like. Until then, it's important to appear at your pitches dressed in a way that shows you care and that you respect the people who have taken time out of their day to meet with you. If in doubt, dress up. You can never go wrong looking too nice, but you can go very wrong looking not nice enough.

Remember to Listen

You probably know more about your product and your market than almost anyone else, but that doesn't mean you know every-thing. Nothing turns buyers (or investors) off more than a know-it-all. While it is admirable to stand firm in your convictions, and you should take every opportunity to offer evidence that sup-ports your claims, don't dismiss buyers' questions or concerns. They have experience and insight that you do not have. If you come across as combative, arrogant, or hardheaded, or buyers see that you're unwilling or incapable of listening to them during a pitch, they're not going to want to work with you, no matter how amazing they find your product. There's always another product they can buy to fill their sales quota.

Sometimes It's Good to Share the Spotlight

In some cases, you won't be able to do the pitch yourself. As discussed earlier, some entrepreneurs just aren't suited for public speaking, and so they bring in a partner to be the face of the product even as they sit close by during the pitch and make themselves available for questions. If you've hired a representative firm, they could pitch your product for you. It can be nerve-wracking to let someone else do your pitch. How could anyone else be as passionate about your product as you?

That's why reps and distributors are usually paid a percentage of the amount of each order they land for you. It creates an incentive, making it as much in their best interest to woo buyers for your product as it is yours. That doesn't mean you have to relinquish all control over your pitch, however. Remember, you always need to be driving the bus. Even if you're shy and you've hired a rep to pitch for you, accompany the rep to the presentation. Speak up when and if needed. No one knows your product better than you do.

THE PRE-PITCH PREP

Your Prototype Is Perfect

Take a good, hard look at your prototype. Is it exactly what it should be? Is it perfect? Not is it perfect in an it's-perfect-except-for-that-teeny-little-detail-you-wish-you-had-thought-of-previously kind of way. I mean, it's perfect in that you look at it, and smile, and think, *This. Is. Perfect.* If so, you're already ahead of a lot of other inventors. In fact, you're avoiding a common mistake that I have committed in the past.

We inventors are passionate people, and sometimes—especially once we've enjoyed a little success and are feeling more confident—we can get so excited about a new idea or product that we can't wait to start sharing it with our buyers, so we can get the ball rolling under it quickly. Yet every time I have let my enthusiasm get ahead of me, I've regretted it. Several times I have been so eager to start sharing new ideas at QVC that I have pitched them before they were fully fleshed out. I've learned that you should always make sure the design and the prototype are perfect before revealing it. Don't show it before it's ready and blow your one and only chance to make a good first impression.

Learn from my mistake (the one I never make anymore): Perfect your product so that you can pitch it in all its shining glory, so your buyer can't help falling in love with it.

Your Props Are Ready

Make sure that you've got everything you need to make an unforgettable demonstration. If you need to build a doorway to show how your product hangs off of it, build a portable doorway. If you need to demonstrate how well your product cleans, devise a portable bathtub, kitchen floor, or stovetop, as Aaron Krause did to show that his scrubby sponge was unparalleled at getting the gunk off delicate surfaces. Whatever it takes, do it and do it right! Don't skimp. This saying is true: you have to spend money to make money. Always go out with your best foot forward. You get one shot, so make sure it's perfect.

You Set Your Goals

So, you're confident that your prototype is in its absolute final, perfect incarnation, and you've got your props ready to help you demo your invention. You're ready to start pitching. But there are millions of retailers and buyers out there. Where to begin?

I always had the theory that it was best to go with the biggest retailers with the most stores, for that would get me the highest amount of purchase orders in the shortest amount of time. Not every retail outlet will be appropriate for your product, but don't eliminate retailers because they're too small or you don't think they have the appropriate cachet. Don't worry about cachet. Get in the door and be grateful to anyone who is willing to take a chance on you. Do what you must to get your start. Don't let anyone take advantage of you, but you should be willing to put up with a lot in order to get your foot in the door. It's a rite of passage we all take.

Realistically, you may know that it's unlikely you're going to get a multimillion-dollar contract with a large national chain right out of the gate. But at this point, it's only unlikely, not impossible. Go big. Go fast and furious. Here's what I say all the time: Cast as wide a net as you can. Do not be intimidated. Knock on every door, call every phone number, and write to every email address you can possibly find belonging to a buyer that might be interested in what you're selling. What have you got to lose? Everything! Don't let fear, laziness, or a lack of persistence keep you from getting an audience with the people who are guarding the gates to your future. And do not turn down sales; a bird in the hand is valuable.

I recently did a deal with three guys from New Jersey who had invented a simple plastic case that would keep flat paintbrushes and roller brushes wet—The Paintbrush Cover. No more furiously washing the brushes at the end of every day to keep them from drying out and getting ruined. The case keeps the brushes moist for months and months. It's patented, too! These three represented everything I look for in an entrepreneur. They were burning with enthusiasm. They flew out to California, and the morning of their *Shark Tank* appearance, instead of practicing their pitch or pacing their hotel rooms nervously, they went out and knocked on the doors of a few hardware stores. And as they proudly declared on air, each one bought!

It was with that sort of determination that I set out to get my first invention into every single retail store where it belonged. Every night, after spending all day polling women on the streets of Chicago, I'd sit with the book I had lugged home from the library (it cost about a thousand dollars!). It was called *The Department Store Guide*, and it was the best tool ever. I'd scour it and select the top stores I wanted to target. All of them were the ones with the largest number of stores. I'd make endless lists in my notebooks. I copied every relevant name and phone number I could find.

Today you might use a publication called *The Chain Store Guide*, which provides a comprehensive list of retailers across the country and the names of their most important personnel. The information is also online at www.chainstoreguide.com.

My plan was to go big—so big that it might have seemed unreasonable to anyone but me: my product was well suited for any store, so I was going to reach out to every single one, beginning with the largest chains with the most stores. I was sure that if I could start selling into four or five of the top retailers in the country, I would make my entry into all the other retailers.

START WITH A FAST PITCH

I was sure that if I could get buyers on the phone for just a few minutes, and give them a taste of my energy and excitement, and how great my product was, they would be curious enough to agree to meet with me in person. My phone was equipped with speed redial, so every day I would start at the top of my list and call the first number. If no one picked up or I got to voice mail,

I'd hang up and immediately redial. If no one picked up or I got to voice mail, I'd redial again. If still no response, I'd wait an hour and hit redial again. I'd try every hour or so. I didn't want the individual to be irritated when he or she picked up. There was no caller ID back then, which helped. This system was frustrating, and it was boring, but it worked. Sometimes it took hours, but someone would eventually pick up. And every time someone did, I hit the person with a brief yet extremely precise introduction, carefully scripted to pique his or her interest.

The Script

Buyers are just like everyone else—busy, overscheduled with meetings, and stressed out about their sales goals. They don't have time to be interrupted unless it is by something or someone who will make their sales goals easier to hit, their workday better, and their bosses happy. So with every word I spoke, I tried to convey the message that that's exactly what I had to offer. I knew there would be no time for introductions or for polite chitchat (though I was exceedingly polite). I had to capture the person's attention with one catchy, appealing sentence. So my opening sentence was, "Hi, my name is Lori Greiner. I have a revolutionary new product and you've never seen anything like it."

If the person didn't hang up on me right away, I went on with what could best be described as a mini-pitch: "It's the coolest earring organizer ever. It holds 100 pair of pierced and clip-on earrings on sliding earring stands. The stands slide to the left and to the right, one behind the other, and it takes up only about nine inches of space on your dresser. I'm going to be in your city in two weeks. Would you have just five minutes for me to quickly show it to you? I think you will love it. I promise I'll set my watch, and in five minutes I'll leave if you want."

See how concise I was? No filler, no unnecessary information, nothing except the main things every buyer needs to hear before he or she will even think about giving you a chance to make a pitch:

1. That you've got a brand-new, original product people will love.

2. That it is exciting.

3. That you will be quick and easy to work with.

4. That you are ready to meet at their convenience.

Take a close look at the words I used. Each sentence was important: "I have a revolutionary new product . . ." "It holds one hundred pair . . ." "It takes up only nine inches . . ." I struck their imaginations. I also said there was nothing on the market like it.

The trick is to be quick, likeable, and assertive but not aggressive.

If a buyer's immediate response is no, you can reply with, "I promise you this is different from anything you've seen before. Please, just five minutes?" Stay polite and respectful at all times. And then stop. Don't keep pushing, because then you'll become annoying, and no one wants to do business with someone who is annoying.

If the person tells you send pictures or information via email, say that the product will really come to life when he or she can see the real thing. You're always more convincing in person. You'll be too easy to dismiss if you're just one more blip in an inbox, so do whatever you can to get a face-to-face meeting.

The Email Pitch

I tell my entrepreneurs all the time that when calling a buyer, they should speak in short, quick, and precise sentences, because people are busy and won't listen past a few sentences. This advice holds true for email, as well as phone pitches. In fact, often it may be more common for you to reach buyers by email than by phone, since that's how people communicate in business. But the process isn't that different. Your emails should be short and concise.

People don't read past the first few sentences, so grab their attention fast. You need to edit, edit, and edit your emails again before sending them out. I do it (and I encourage my *Shark Tank* entrepreneurs to do it, too). I'll write out all my thoughts, and then ruthlessly shorten them. No one wants to read through a whole bunch of stuff. Also, people love bullet points. If you want people to read your email, don't write big run-on paragraphs. There is nothing worse, and people will click away. I do.

Do something in your email to catch people's attention and stand out. If you're comfortable with revealing your product, embed an image of it so buyers can immediately see why you're so excited, or send an attachment or a link to a product page, especially to a YouTube video or a video on your website that demonstrates and shows the product so that they can instantly see why it's wonderful. You might win them over in those few seconds.

That's what happened when a bright young college student named Angela, from Boston, was passed through to my website after taking my Hero or Zero app test. She sent me a quick, concise submittal with her idea for a makeup brush that opened in the middle and held four more brushes inside. She included drawings of the product. The email captured our attention instantly. I called her and we did the product together. I manufactured it for her, we launched it on QVC, and it was a success. And Angela is a happy lady today.

At the rate people skim emails, the more you can reveal up front, the more likely you are to grab their attention. You probably know this from experience. When you're busy and in a hurry, it can seem like too much work to bother clicking to open an attachment or a link. Make it as easy as possible for buyers to see everything they need to see in one quick glance. People are glutted with information, so make your email short, memorable, and visually enticing.

That said, try to capture a buyer on the phone so that you can use your power of persuasion. Emails are great for pictures, but not so good for expressing tone or emotion. I still believe in the power of a phone call and the live human voice. It is supremely easy to delete or ignore an email without even opening it, just because you don't recognize the name of the sender or you don't like the subject line. Most people, however, have to listen to the whole first sentence of a phone call before they can determine whether they want to continue the conversation or not. If your first sentence is powerful and intriguing enough— and makes it clear that listening might offer your buyer an edge at work—you might get to finish your introduction and schedule a face-to-face meeting.

RISK PAYS OFF

Now, I was calling buyers all over the country and asking for appointments when I didn't have a single plane ticket purchased. But no one needed to know that. If a buyer sounded willing to meet with me but was unavailable the week I offered to come in, I'd tell the buyer that I had another trip scheduled two weeks after that. No matter what he or she said, I had an answer. I made it so easy that the person couldn't come up with an excuse not to meet me. If the buyer didn't want to hear my pitch, he or she was going to have to flat-out say so. But very few people did.

There are probably a few reasons for this. First, my product was easy to visualize, and what I was describing really was unlike anything these buyers had ever seen. Second, when you are polished, determined, and persistent, most buyers start to get curious. What if you're the real deal? What if you really do have the next big thing? They don't want to miss out, and if your mini pitch is just right, they may have reason to believe that you might just be worth a few more minutes of their time. And if you've got a brilliant product and a brilliant pitch, a few minutes of face-to-face time is all you'll need to seal the deal.

As a result of those incessant phone calls and my tightly wound pitch, I ended up traveling to nineteen cities in twenty-one days. I was in Ohio one day, Texas the next, Arkansas after that. It was exhausting. And although I traveled as cheaply as possible, taking low-budget airlines and many connecting flights, I knew I was risking a lot of money on flights to go to meetings that might not come to anything. But the risk paid off, because ultimately most of the buyers I was fortunate enough to get a meeting with gave me a chance.

PITCH TO-DO LIST:

❏ Perfect your prototype.

❏ Compile the contact information for every buyer at every intended retailer.

❏ Write a cold-call script that you can say quickly.

❏ Write an email that will capture people's attention right away.

❏ Know every detail about your product.

❏ Be able to outline your product's features and benefits.

❏ Be able to explain why it is an exciting, brand-new, original product that people will love.

❏ Reassure them that you will be easy to work with.

❏ Make it as easy as possible for them to meet with you.

❏ Write a pitch that can answer all the questions buyers will likely ask.

❏ Practice your pitch over, and over, and over again.

8

THE DREAM BECOMES TANGIBLE— MANUFACTURING AND PACKAGING

"Quality means doing it right when no one is looking."
—Henry Ford

THERE IS NOTHING MORE EXCITING TO A NEW ENTREPRENEUR than getting that first purchase order (PO). Finally, there's hard proof that someone other than your mother agrees with you that there is a hole in the market to be filled and that people will be willing, even eager, to spend money on your brainchild. There's proof that all the planning and research and phone calls and hope and work haven't been in pursuit of some pipe dream. When your PO comes in, you'll want to have a manufacturer already lined up so that when you say the word, a factory foreman merely has to hit the start button to get your production lines rolling. As with almost every step in the invention-to-market process, however, getting to this point takes significant effort and research.

CHOOSING A MANUFACTURER

Where you make your product can be a complicated and, for some, even a morally fraught decision. If it is important to you to be able to personally supervise operations as your product comes off the line—it was for me—your first instinct will be to try to manufacture your product locally. Today, unfortunately, many manufacturers have shut down in the United States or have moved their operations overseas, and many product categories are almost exclusively produced in China or India.

Many entrepreneurs feel strongly about supporting local businesses, and also believe that the "Made in America" label will serve as a major selling point. I wholeheartedly support that belief and say go with it if you can. Sometimes, however, you may discover when starting out that despite your best intentions, it may not be possible for the type of business you're in. I made everything in the United States for many years, but when I decided to make products out of wood, that became impossible. The manufacturing costs in the United States are often higher than they would be in Asia, India, or anyplace else overseas. Fortunately, in recent years we have seen some change. For some types of products, however, it may remain harder to hit the prices the public wants while trying to manufacture in the United States.

Manufacturing close to home can sometimes make it extremely difficult to make a profit on some products, because you can only charge so much, and if your manufacturing costs are too high, you're not going to make enough money to sustain and grow the company, which in turn is not good for your local economy. If you find this is the case, use overseas production if you need to, with the goal of bringing your manufacturing back home as soon as you can. Having a successful, thriving business will allow

> Even if you are manufacturing overseas, you should feel positive about the fact that by growing a business here and doing what's best for it, you will also be providing American workers with employment and contributing to economic growth.

you to employ more Americans and use American resources for everything else, such as your employees, warehousing, your attorneys, your graphic designers, photographers, sales team, and so on. You can put a lot of Americans to work even if you cannot manufacture in the U.S.A. Another way companies sometimes try to keep their costs in check while still doing as much business as possible in the United States is by making some parts overseas and assembling them here. I am happy to say that many of my *Shark Tank* entrepreneurs have found such great success since we made our deal that they now employ many Americans.

Selecting a manufacturer will be an extremely personal decision you have to make. However, your main concern should ultimately be the same wherever your manufacturer is located—upholding your standards of quality and safety while keeping your product's price point at a level that makes it attractive to customers.

What to Consider

First, what type of factory makes your type of product? Is your product made out of plastic, metal, glass, wood, or textiles, to name a few materials? Every factory specializes in a product category, but over time they often develop a reputation for excelling in a particular niche. For example, both a travel bag and a purse are in a category called "cut and sew." But if you have designed a new piece of luggage, ideally you would want to work with a manufacturer that produces luggage, not handbags. Whenever possible, select suppliers who have experience working with products like yours. Ask for recommendations from people you meet in the industry, such as your prototype maker, or people you might interact with at trade shows. There are a host of rules specific to every industry, and you want to be sure you're working with a factory that understands them all and knows how to make a product compliant with laws, rules, and regulations.

Next, once you locate the factories nearest you that can handle your product, look up their credentials and any online reviews. Look for their Better Business Bureau ratings. Call the factory and ask for references. Inquire about their other clients (if they haven't signed confidentiality agreements), look up the products they make, and read the customer reviews. I once chose a manufacturer because I found out they made bags for Donna Karan, reasoning that it must be a reliable and quality manufacturer if it was working for such a big, quality brand. On the flip side, should you notice that several of the products manufactured at a factory are frequently panned online for being low quality, defective, or otherwise subpar, take heed.

If you can find a manufacturer you'd like to work with close to home, pay a visit in person. Ask to see the production lines and examine the quality of what is being made. Are you impressed? Does the product look nice? Does it work? Introduce yourself to the factory owners and ask to meet the head foreman. Do your instincts tell you that these would be ethical, responsible people to work with? Do they seem to care about the products they're making and the people working for them? Do you get a sense that they would be willing to solve problems creatively, and would be responsive when faced with a dilemma? Make sure you let them know that if you decide to do business together, they can expect to see you often because you intend to be as involved as possible in the production process.

These on-site visits are one of the best ways for a new entrepreneur to grow and learn about manufacturing, and it helps you creatively when you're coming up with your next great idea. As you watch and learn, and spend time around the manufacturing process, you become more aware of what types of processes are available. As I learned about injection molding, I also learned about extruding and thermoforming. I learned that you could add wood chips to plastic to mimic the look of wood. I learned about colors and colorants. You just learn so much more on site than you would if your manufacturer were located overseas.

Manufacturing Overseas

Sometimes, however, there won't be any manufacturers you can work with in your area, or you will calculate that, for the sake of cost efficiency, you will have to produce overseas. However, bear in mind that when you manufacture overseas, you trade lower costs for higher risk, because you won't be able to keep as close an eye on the production process.

You'll look for an overseas manufacturer much the same way as you would one that's local. Get recommendations from people in the know, especially from retailers. Check the international company's credentials. To my knowledge there is no international equivalent to the Better

BureauVeritas: www.bureauveritas.com

Intertek: www.intertek.com

SGS: www.sgsgroup.us.com

Business Bureau, but testing labs like Bureau Veritas, Intertek, and SGS can do a factory audit and tell you if the factory is okay or not.

You can even hire a representative to select a manufacturer for you and negotiate pricing for your order. Often these manufacturer's reps receive a 5 to 10 percent commission, or they will tack 10 to 15 percent onto the cost of the goods from the factory if they act as your direct source. For that kind of money, however, they should do far more than just make the connection between you and a reputable manufacturer. They should also do inspections, going in even before production begins to confirm that the manufacturer is not using child labor, that working conditions are good, and that you will be getting a high-quality product. Before the product ships, they should also visit and check that your product is being made and packaged correctly, according to the specifications you've given or that your retailer has given to you.

In addition to your representatives, you can also hire the same labs to send out an independent third-party inspector. They are invaluable, especially if you're placing a sizable order. I use them all the time to check on big orders, even at factories where I've been doing business for years. They visit the manufacturers and make sure that the order coming off the line meets the standards you expect and are compliant with safety and environmental regulations. These regulations vary from country to country, so you have to be extremely careful when selling internationally.

The representatives can provide you with lists of regulations and the safety laws you need to follow, and they will know what you need to do so that your product is compliant. Wood products have to be properly sourced; many fabrics need to be treated with flame-retardants; certain adhesives and aerosol coatings once allowed are now banned. Even though the regulations gov-

> **Start by visiting the Consumer Product Safety
> Commission website. It's packed with information
> for consumers, businesses, and manufacturers alike.
> Also study California's Proposition 65. California is
> aggressive about regulations and has the strictest
> restrictions regarding cancer-causing materials and
> chemicals of any state in the country. Prop 65 was
> an initiative that required California to post a list of
> cancer-causing materials and update it every year.
> Check to see if anything used for your product is
> included on that list. If your product can pass
> inspection in California, it can probably pass
> inspection anywhere else.**

erning the use of these materials can seem indecipherable, you
need to understand them thoroughly, and make sure you stay up
to date, as they change over time. It would be horrible to think
you're ready to sell and suddenly be told that you have to make
changes if you want to be compliant with regulatory codes because you're using a dye that's just been declared illegal, or your
product poses a risk to children, or your instruction sheet has to
be rewritten. Similarly, a washing and care instruction label is
required on countless items, from T-shirts to travel bags, and if
you didn't have one, you'd have to go back and get one sewn in.

Fortunately, upon placing an order, many retailers will give
you a terms and conditions guidebook that generally includes a
list of manufacturing guidelines that must be met if you want
to sell in their stores. You need to make sure that you meet all
of their requirements, not just so that you can build a good re-

lationship with the store but also because noncompliance usually results in your being required to pay regulatory fines. In the worst-case scenario, you could be forced to take your product off the market until the issue is resolved.

How can you make sure your product passes inspection? Most of the time your retailers will give you quality assurance guidelines, and sometimes they'll identify an issue and help you find specific help to address it. Ultimately, though, the responsibility to comply with rules and regulations falls on your shoulders.

QUALITY CONTROL IS YOUR JOB

Manufacturers generally ask their clients to pay 20 or 30 percent down upon signing a contract, with the rest due upon shipping. You want to know about any manufacturing imperfections before the order leaves the port or for the stores, because once your product ships, it will be too late to fix the problem and you'll still be required to pay your remaining balance. Hire an inspection team to pull a percentage of your units at random from the production line. You tell the inspectors what to check—color, stitching, finish, joints, any relevant production details—and how much of a "tolerance" you will have for defects.

Tolerance for Defects

Most people set their tolerance levels at plus or minus 1 percent, giving the run a small amount of wiggle room for minor issues like tiny dirt spots or color that's marginally off. So if your inspector pulls fifteen samples of your product and finds that there is only a small dirt spot or one loose thread on one item out of those fifteen, that's a good indication that the production run overall meets your standards of quality. If the inspector notices that nine out of the fifteen samples have a zipper that catches rather than glides smoothly back and forth, that's a reliable indicator that there's a problem with the entire batch.

Now you can show your factory the inspection results and demand that they fix the problem. You have leverage because you're under no obligation to pay your balance until the product ships, so it's in the factory's best interest to comply. Don't ever turn your back on your product, no matter how good your relationship is with your manufacturer. You have got to keep your eyes open (in person or through an inspection team) because no matter how good your relationship is with your manufacturer, glitches will happen. And when they do, you want to make sure that you aren't forced to eat the cost of someone else's mistake.

The Aches and Pains of Expansion

I began manufacturing overseas somewhat reluctantly, and in the beginning it was an extremely bumpy ride. For the first five years of my career I had exclusively created my consumer products out of plastic and made them all in Chicago. I did pay more than I would have had I gone overseas, but I liked that my products were being made in the United States, and that I was able to be at the factory all the time watching, learning, and making sure my products were good quality.

I owned close to thirty-five molds and was making over twenty-five successfully selling products. I was on a prolific creative roll. Then I realized it was time to start making things out of wood—that was just the natural next progression for me. I designed a new wooden jewelry box that I called the Gold and Silver Safekeeper. Unfortunately, I discovered that it would be extremely cost-prohibitive to make it in the United States. I sent my sample to several U.S. manufacturers to get quotes, but the same jewelry box I could make in China for $45 would have *cost* me $200-$250 to make it in the United States because of the intensive labor, the parts, and the intricacies involved. I needed to make the product overseas or it would fail.

Then something exciting happened. QVC saw my prototype and selected it to be a "Today's Special Value" (TSV) for November. A TSV is a product specially featured for a select twenty-four hours at a special low price that day only. November was the best selling time of the year. It was a spot that everyone who sold at QVC coveted, and I was ecstatic. I had no connections to overseas manufacturers, so QVC paired me up with a supplier they had worked with before. I had learned so much about dealing with American manufacturing, but now I needed to understand a whole new international regulatory and tariff system.

My jewelry boxes have an antitarnish lining that is made in the United States, which meant that the lining would have to be exported to China in order to be assembled into the boxes, then imported back into the United States in the finished product. That posed an unexpected problem. Factories have to have special licenses and quotas in order to export something into China only to export it back out again. It's not something that's

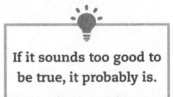

If it sounds too good to be true, it probably is.

done often, so though he had been doing business for years, this new supplier didn't know he needed the license, nor how to get one. Now I was stuck. We needed to start manufacturing to make delivery on time for a November TSV, and time was running out. The TSV was a big deal to us and to QVC, my biggest customer, so everyone was in a bit of a panic.

QVC had a vendor whom I'll call Louis. Hearing about our situation, Louis told my director at QVC that he would do us all a favor and help me get the product made at no profit to him. Those were his words: no profit.

I asked Louis to sign a confidentiality noncompete agreement, which he promised he would do, but he urged me to immediately send him my sample overnight because his supplier from China was in his U.S. office for one day only and was leaving in the morning, and they needed to see the product. I was not comfortable with this. Normally I would never send samples of a brand-new product to get a manufacturing quote without first getting a signed confidentiality noncompete. I told him I'd prefer that he sign it now. He said there was no time—it was 8 p.m., and I had one hour to get the box to FedEx before it closed. He promised he

Don't ever, EVER, do anything against your better judgment.

would sign in the morning. This TSV opportunity was a big deal to me, so against my better judgment I sent the sample without his signature.

This supplier was a bad guy. He never sent back my confidentiality noncompete. He strung me along for weeks without showing me a sample. Two months later, he also had never signed our sourcing agreement, a document I send to all my suppliers and that people typically sign within a few days. He'd send it to me without redlining any of the changes he had made, which is highly unethical and forced my attorney and me to spend hours rereading the entire document every time it came back to us. We spent two months going back and forth over this document. I was trying to stick with him because the TSV was such a big deal to me and to my vice president and director at QVC.

The final straw came when he sent me back a final agreement stating that he would be the sole manufacturer not only for this jewelry box but also for any jewelry box I made in the future, and that I would only make a nickel per box! This from the man who had said he would help QVC and me as a favor, for no profit.

That's when I called the VP at QVC, explained what happened, and told him that I had to pull out of the TSV because I couldn't sell my soul to the devil. He understood.

I lost that wonderful pre-holiday spot, and by the end of the entire fiasco I was out $50,000 in legal fees. But proving my theory that the worst things that happen to us are often blessings in disguise, three great things happened as a result of this awful experience:

1. Right after, I met a supplier who did sign my confidentiality noncompete and we went on to make hundreds of products together.

2. That supplier, John, became a dear friend.

3. The following year, QVC selected the jewelry box for their November TSV, placing an even higher order than the year before.

FEW PEOPLE REALIZE HOW COMPLICATED it can be to produce even a relatively simple-looking product. Dan and I eventually went to China to visit the factory where our wood full-length mirrored jewelry cabinets are made, and what we saw was impressive, even for us who were familiar with manufacturing processes. Every piece of the product— the frame, the earring bars, the bracelet bars, the necklace bars,

> "The strongest swords are forged in the hottest fires."
> —CHINESE PROVERB

the mirrors—are separate pieces that are made first and then assembled. Each has to be cut, stained, dried, and recoated, one at a time. Then there's the frame for the entire cabinet, which measures 60 x 3 x 14 inches. Once a frame is painted, the workers hang the piece on a giant hook attached to an overhead conveyer belt. Imagine walking into a factory the size of three football fields and looking up to see a merry-go-round system like what you might see at the dry cleaner's, spinning these large cabinets around in a circle above your head. There's no place to store them, so they just stay up there until they're dry and ready to be removed for final assembly.

When we told the factory to make 40,000 of these mirrored jewelry cabinets, we could not imagine the scale such an order represented and how much space it would require. The product required many steps to assemble, from connecting the mirror to the frame, to lining the interior with antitarnish fabric, to inserting all the pieces inside that hold the jewelry—not to mention the sanding, the staining, and the thousands of packaging boxes. It was impressively well orchestrated and organized. People don't realize what is involved in making many of the products they use every day. I was in awe.

PACKAGING

You want to work with a reputable, responsible manufacturer because you want to make sure that your customers have the best possible experience when they buy your product. But equally important is the experience your customers have with your product before the point of purchase. Your packaging is a stand-in for you, selling your product when you're not around to demonstrate and explain its qualities and benefits. In the same way that the opening line of your pitch must be carefully crafted to engage and intrigue a buyer or investor, your package must telegraph everything you want people to know about your product—in a single glance. It is what speaks to your consumer at the moment of truth, the point of sale, when consumers stand in front of a retail shelf and see your product lined up along with all the other competitors vying for attention. It should say, "Me. Choose me. I'm just what you need. Here's why."

Package design is a science, tapping into human emotions and even reinforcing consumers' feelings about themselves. Tools are usually packaged in such a way that whoever picks them up feels a little bit handier, a little more confident that they really can build that deck in the backyard. Computers, mobile devices, and their respective accessories are often sleek and compact, appealing to a contemporary, minimalist aesthetic that makes buyers feel like they're just a little bit cooler than they were before they made their purchase. Cosmetic and fragrance companies spend a fortune designing packaging that makes women feel beautiful and elegant when they buy a jar of cream or a bottle of perfume.

Everything about your packaging, from its size and shape, to the colors, to the image on the front, to the text and its placement, and even the font, will matter, and will have to convey your product's key selling points like a shot to your consumers' heart.

Types of Packaging

There are several types of packaging. In brick-and-mortar stores, you generally see small consumer goods packaged on hangtags, in clamshells, or blister packs that hang off of rods, while larger items like vacuum cleaners, food processors, or jewelry boxes come in four-color boxes that reside on shelves. The designs of these boxes often follow the same general formula: a big image of the product, a brand name, and a description.

Key to great packaging is gorgeous, informative visuals that immediately convey what your product is and how it works. Be careful not to add too many bells and whistles that could distract from your product, which should be the star of the show. Text should be clear and punchy. Do not expect anyone to read more than a few words. Your text is there to supplement your visuals and explain your value proposition in a way that a picture of your product cannot. Less is more nowadays, and frequently consumer brands are creating beautiful, sophisticated packaging that speaks volumes with very little text.

You can send a powerful message about the product inside the box with a bright punch of color or minimalist white, or a playful or dramatic font. A clever shape can get you noticed, but it can also work against you. For example, *Shark Tank* entrepreneurs Hanna and Mark Lim met with initial enthusiasm from big-box stores for their innovative sippy cup, but then ran into a problem when the stores questioned whether the cute but folded-paper-bag-shaped packaging would allow them to fit enough product on the shelves. Jordan Eisenberg, founder of UrgentRX, had to get creative to solve a problem caused by his product's unusual packaging. His single-dose packets of flavored, powdered versions of over-the-counter medicines couldn't get placement in pharmacies until he created his own, custom-made display units that took advantage of unused space at the checkout counter.

As always, you have to do your research when deciding what kind of packaging to use. Visit the retailers that sell to your market and look at what styles are currently popular. What appeals to you? What catches your eye? Big brands pay hundreds of thousands of market research dollars when designing their packaging; you can learn from them and their packaging and see how they marketed the products, what colors they used, what images, and what style. Analyze why the packaging was appealing to you or why it caught your eye.

While you don't want to copy them, you should pay attention to what they're doing and why they use the style they do to sell the product inside. For example, often they will use a large photo of the product to explain what it is instead of a lot of wording. There's a reason for that: people don't take the time to read a lot of words on packages. They need to be able to see the product and immediately understand it. They don't like busy packaging with a lot going on and lots of text; they just won't take the time to decipher it.

My philosophy is that packaging should be clean and use great images to tell the product's story. I imagine myself rushing down the aisle and I think: *What caught my attention on the shelf? What did I notice? Did I instantly understand what the product is? Did it make me want to buy it?*

As discussed, historically, retailers didn't like dealing with inventors selling just one SKU, but recently stores are showing more willingness to work with entrepreneurs, going so far as to develop initiatives to help get them started. Walmart, for example, started the Get on the Shelf contest, and QVC has the Sprouts program. Retailers can often recommend packagers, and in turn the packagers will probably give you the names of printers with whom they do business.

Package Design

When it comes to actually designing your packaging, unless you have a graphic design background, you'll want to hire a professional to help you create something unique, enticing, and effective. Get referrals if you can. If not, most graphic designers have their portfolios available for review on the Internet. Try to choose one with experience in package design, although expect the fee to be on the high end if you hire someone who has designed for very successful big brands and products. If you are on a budget, you could also opt to work with a crowdsourcing company, such as DesignCrowd, that allows you to post your project and receive bids from designers around the world. The Internet can give you access to fantastic talent at extremely affordable rates. The disadvantage, of course, is that more often than not you won't be able to meet your designer in person. Regardless, the most important thing to look for in graphic designers, besides talent, is whether they understand your product and seem excited and intrigued by it.

Once you hire your photographer and graphic designer, make sure you are clear about your vision. It's very hard for graphic designers and artists to work when they don't have any idea what you want. Being specific makes their jobs easier. In addition, time is money, and if you don't stay involved, your designers may inadvertently take things in a direction you didn't want to go, and then you'll have to start all over again. That can cost you dearly. I trusted my designers, but I stayed close by while they worked, attending the photo shoots, propping my organizer with earrings, offering my thoughts on design, layout, and even fonts. I was on a budget, so I hired a relative newcomer to the field who had an impressive portfolio but little experience with packaging. She did a good job, but because she hadn't yet been around the block enough to recognize red flags, she couldn't anticipate what was coming next.

It took me hours to select and hang all the beautiful earrings on the organizer when I was preparing it for the packaging photo shoot. I used all of my own stuff so I wouldn't have to buy fifty new pair of earrings. Since my organizer was clear plastic, I thought setting it against a dark background would make it pop. I told the graphic designer to design a black box. The end result was striking—the clear organizer looked beautiful against the glossy black background. The problem was that none of us knew that it is extremely risky to work with so much black ink. Any print job saturated with such a heavy concentration of color has a tendency to bleed, black worst of all. Unfortunately, that's exactly what happened when the press operator wasn't paying attention during the print run.

I managed to get the problem resolved (the details of that story appear in Chapter 9), but from then on, at least in the early days, every time the printer would do a run, I would stand by the printing press and watch the first sheets that came out to make sure the colors were true. I would sign off on one sheet that the printer kept, and I would take another one with me. This way, we would both have a sample to refer to for the remainder of the print run. We also do this to this day with product samples. They're never perfect the first time around. Once I get a first sample, I offer my feedback about what changes are needed. We go through several rounds to perfect the sample before it's finalized. Once I've approved the final sample, my supplier keeps one, I keep one, and that's the sample the rest of the production should match.

Eventually, when your business is big enough, you will be able to hire someone to supervise production; and obviously if you are manufacturing overseas, this will be a job for the representative you hire to advocate on your behalf. But in the beginning, whenever you can, try to be present at every stage of production so that you can get a feel for how the process works and what problems to look out for.

This is a common practice in manufacturing that ensures

consistency. I learned my lesson from that printing disaster, and my team knows to have the printer send us a proof before running a print job to make sure the colors are right. For the record, once we used up our thousands of black boxes, we switched the color to much lighter lavender blue, which eliminated the possibility of the problems we'd faced with the black ink. In addition, by then I had decided the lavender was an even more attractive color to the female eye.

Packaging Specifications

You won't even necessarily need a four-color box if your product is going to be sold online or through television channels. On QVC, for example, it's the demonstrability of a product that sells a product, not the aesthetic of its packaging. But anything that will travel through the mail or UPS will need to be packaged in a drop-shippable box that can pass an eleven-point drop test: your product can be picked up and dropped eleven times from a distance of thirty inches onto a concrete surface, landing on all corners, flat surfaces, and two edges, and not suffer any damage. These plain brown corrugated cartons vary in size and are measured in the number of "flutes" per linear foot. The most common one used for shipping purposes is the C-flute. Your packager should be able to advise you on the best packaging option for your product, including whether to include additional immobilizers such as Styrofoam endcaps, bubble wrap, or foam peanuts.

Your retailer's manual should explain all packaging and shipping requirements. QVC has a notoriously stringent quality assurance department that will not allow a purchase order to go through until it has met all requirements, such as passing the eleven-point drop test, displaying all proper labels, and exhibiting all documentation that the product complies with necessary rules and regulations. Of course, they also insist on trying your product and making sure that it works the way you say it will, and that it is in good condition and will leave their customers more than satisfied.

Above all, be true to yourself. You want to be proud of every aspect of your invention. Don't settle until you're satisfied that your manufacturer, your designer, your printer, and your packager are all working together to make your product look its absolute best.

MANUFACTURING AND PACKAGING TO-DO LIST:

- ❑ Compile a list of manufacturers with good reputations for producing goods in your product category.
- ❑ If producing locally, make appointments to visit and meet with the individuals who would be in charge of your product.
- ❑ If producing overseas, contact testing labs to see if the factory you're interested in is in good standing and is socially responsible.
- ❑ Look for a representative who can source your product and negotiate on your behalf.
- ❑ Come up with a clear vision for how you want your packaging to look (but remain open to suggestions).
- ❑ Research and hire a graphic designer and photographer to create your packaging's design.
- ❑ Work with a packaging company to make sure your package will secure your goods and pass an eleven-point drop test, if needed.

9

DRIVING THE BUSINESS

"Nothing is impossible; the word itself says, 'I'm possible.'"
—AUDREY HEPBURN

THE PHONE CALL THAT REALLY CHANGED EVERYTHING FOR ME was the one I made to the corporate offices of JCPenney, in Plano, Texas. There, I spoke with an extraordinarily nice man named Paul Clark. He listened to what I had to say. I did my fast pitch, and said, "I'll be in Plano next week," and I asked him if he could meet with me at his office at JCPenney headquarters. Days later, I was standing in his office, demonstrating how my earring organizer worked and pitching with everything I had. When I was done, he informed me that he loved my product, but that each individual JCPenney buyer made his or her own purchasing decisions (the retailer's buying policy has since changed).

Then he made me a deal: if I could sell my organizer into all twelve JCPenney stores in the Chicagoland area, and it did well in the fourth quarter, which is October, November, and December, he would take it nationwide. It was August. Fourth-quarter orders are usually put to bed in April. After thanking Paul Clark, I left his office so excited, because I knew no matter what, I was going to meet his challenge and get into every Chicagoland store. The next day I started calling.

I called every single JCPenney store within a 100-mile radius. I did my mini-pitch over the phone, those same sentences—"Hi, I'm Lori Greiner. I have the coolest earring organizer ever!"— same as always, with the added line that I had met with Paul Clark in Plano headquarters, and he thought I had something they would want to see. I got my appointments, I did my pitch, and every single store bought.

YOU'RE NEVER DONE

Now I had to make sure that sales were so good that Paul would jump at the chance to take me nationwide. All I was required to do was ship my product to the stores and wait for the sales results, but there was no way I was going to stand idly by and hope for the best. Surely there was something else I could do to ensure that everyone who walked past a display of the Earring Organizer would stop to take a closer look.

I decided that the best way to sell the organizer was to show everyone what it could do. It was a hard product to display because clear polystyrene is transparent and doesn't show well on its own. I hung the prototype with fifty pair of beautiful color-coordinated earrings in all styles and sizes, and every weekend I would bring it into two of the stores in the Chicagoland area. I'd spend Saturday in downtown Chicago and Sunday in Schaumburg. The following weekend I'd spend Saturday in Vernon Hills and Sunday in Buffalo Grove, and so on. I'd find a little spot next to where the store had displayed the organizer, and from the minute the store opened to when they locked the doors at night, I would demo.

Over and over, I would catch people's eyes and say, "Look, isn't this cool?" and I would slide the Lucite stands back and forth, and back and forth, and open the drawer and show them how great it was and why they needed it, or why it would be the greatest gift. It was the coolest earring organizer ever, right! People noticed, and they stopped, and they'd watch me, and then they'd buy. When traffic would slow down, Dan would often sidle up and start exclaiming about how interesting the organizer was, and could I tell him more about it? That would bring people over quickly. People are naturally curious, and no one ever wants to miss out. I sold about 80 to 100 organizers a day, every weekend. I did this throughout the holiday season, and when it was done, I had beaten the quota Paul Clark set for me. He kept his promise to take me nationwide, and that spring my invention was selling in every JCPenney across the country.

My philosophy is that you can do anything if you put your mind to it. Many in the retail industry might say that conceiving, pitching, manufacturing, and shipping a product to stores in a handful of months requires a miracle. But I had no choice. I knew the holiday season was peak sales season, and if I didn't hit it, I'd have to wait a whole additional year. I believed I could make anything happen; I just needed to figure out how. It was hell, but I was so excited I was like a woman possessed. And when the doors did start to open, I didn't slow down—I pushed ahead even harder.

You have to keep driving your business forward. You want to keep your hands on the steering wheel so that when challenges arise or problems occur, you can take it where you need or want to go.

But now I had a problem. I couldn't be in 1,200 stores to demonstrate my product, yet I knew it was important for people to be able to quickly see and understand why it was so cool and unique, and how it worked. Then I realized that, though I couldn't be in every store, a model of the organizer could be. An organizer sitting on the counter with earrings hanging from it would help sell the packaged product and would attract a lot of attention. I went to the craft store, bought thousands of gold-colored beads and jewelry wire, and got to work making pretty but inexpensive pairs of earrings. Mind you, while gold and shiny, they were just plastic balls. No one was going to want to steal them. I hung about eight pair per unit, twisting the jewelry wire around the rods with tweezers so that they couldn't easily fall off.

My fingers killed, I made over one thousand individual earrings for the displays. Then I packaged the store display in its box, taped a big note to the top that said, "Store Display. Please place on jewelry counter," and placed one in every master carton of my product that was heading out to the stores. I did it myself because I felt it was important that every store got their sample, and I was going to kill myself if I found out that all those hours twisting wires with needle-nosed pliers were for nothing because the displays didn't make it out onto the floor. The retailers put the display out and it helped my product sell even though I couldn't be there to do a demo. Dan and I would go to the stores in our area to make sure the displays were out and help from time to time, continuing with an occasional live demo on weekends.

When you get an order, your work should not end with shipping your product to the store. *There is more to be done.* You should check periodically on how your product is displayed, where it's displayed, and that everything is going well. When we get my *Shark Tank* entrepreneurs into the stores, they're always checking to see how their products are displayed and making sure everything is right. And of course, taking photos as a proud parent would. That's what driving the bus looks like. It's about making sure that you've got control over your product, and over your destiny, every step of the way toward accomplishing your goal, which is to sell successfully.

Things got exciting. I expanded from JCPenney and got into Marshall Field's, Linens 'n Things, Kohl's, and Carson Pirie Scott, to name a few, as well as several catalogs along with QVC. I was as excited about each new store we'd land as I had been about the first one.

RELATIONSHIPS MATTER

One of the most important things any entrepreneur, or anyone in business, can do is to get to know the people you work with. It's stunning how few people do this. I suppose that's because it takes time to get to know someone, to find out how many kids they have, what they like to do on the weekends, and what teams they root for. Time is money, and time talking about which is superior, a crusty deep-dish Chicago-style pizza or the thin, flimsier slices preferred in New York, can be time away from the immediate concerns of your business. But it is time well spent—maybe some of the best investment possible.

Because one day you will need to rely on these people to solve a problem, or to help you meet a special order, and they will have a choice. They could choose to step up, maybe beyond the parameters of their job, and make sure your problem is solved; or they could continue on as usual and let you fend for yourself. If you have made their business your business, if you have shown them that you appreciate how hard they work, and have treated them with respect, kindness, and care, there is a much better chance that they will in turn make your business their business and value its success almost as much as you do. Building friendships and finding advocates at every level in a business ensures that when you need them, people are willing to help you fight your battles because they believe in you and want you to succeed. More than once, the effort I put into building relationships helped me avert major crises. In fact, if I hadn't done it, my very first order for JCPenney might have ended in disaster.

A Crisis Averted

The first manufacturer I used was housed in an old factory that had been around for almost a hundred years, one of those places where you can still feel the ghosts of our industrial past and the generations of men and women who worked there. Like many U.S. manufacturers, the company had experienced a slowdown in recent years, so the arrival of my business was welcome. I liked them, they were good guys, and I spent a lot of time talking with them in their offices, learning about the company. I would go down to the factory almost every day, making sure that everything was running smoothly, and building relationships with everyone working on my product, from the foreman to the press operator, to the people packing the product, to the guys fixing the tools in the tool room. In addition, I found that being so involved and learning as much as I could about how the factory worked meant that when things went wrong, I was able to do something about it.

Seeing your finished product come off the line for the first time is such a thrill. Here it is, your baby, the physical embodiment of the idea you've been working toward for so long. I was so excited I couldn't wait for the day my first organizer came off the presses. I stood on the factory floor, at the end of the conveyor belt, and let it roll to me. I picked up the organizer and automatically started moving the stands to see how they slid. And they stuck. This was not good. Plastic often shrinks and expands with heat and pressure, and the molds often need to be tweaked when they're brand-new. That's what had happened here. Not to worry, the toolmaker assured me. It would only take three weeks for him to fix the mold and then my product would be perfect. This was not okay. I didn't have three weeks. I had one week. In one week my product was supposed to be packed and shipped to JCPenney so it could hit the shelves.

Some people think that the best way to get what they want is to pull power trips or get aggressive. But not only is that kind of behavior unnecessary, it's also counterproductive. Even if you have some power, you don't want people to do what you want them to do out of fear or because you're making their life miserable. You want them to work with you to solve a problem because they believe in what you're trying to accomplish, and because they feel like they're part of a team.

When you run into trouble and need to rally the troops, don't pressure people by focusing on the consequences of failure but, rather, on what you could all gain with success.

The factory and the toolmaker understand how purchase orders and retailers work, and they know how critical deadlines are for the holiday season, so I tried to persuade the toolmaker to fix the mold with lightning speed. I pointed out that if the product did well, the factory would do well—I could make more products, and he would make the tools for them. I shared what it would mean if, instead of manufacturing enough product to fill the shelves of twelve JCPenneys, they were manufacturing enough product to fill the shelves of hundreds of JCPenneys, in addition to the other smaller retailers that were already about to carry my organizer. How much more profit would that translate into? How many more hours could they offer their employees? How many more jobs could they provide to the community?

I didn't ask him to bend over backward for me out of the goodness of his heart; I asked him to help me because, if we could get this done, we would all win. And on top of that, I begged. He knew I was a brand-new entrepreneur, and he realized how much this new business meant to all of us. This was my first product order, and if anything went wrong I might never get another chance like this again. I laid my heart out and appealed to his sense of compassion. He got it, and the tool was fixed in a week.

> **The power of persuasion lies in making people understand the big picture.**

Always explain to people why you are asking them to do things for you, especially when you are asking them to rush an order or go out of their way. No one likes to be ordered around, but when people understand why you're saying, "I need this to-morrow," or "Get it done in two weeks," they're often willing to help you drive the bus. This kind of communication and trust building is an important element in business.

Be Proactive to Solve Problems

That wasn't the end of my problems, unfortunately. As the mold was being tweaked, the first shipment of boxes arrived so that the factory workers could start packaging the organizers and load-ing them into master cartons to be shipped out to warehouses. One look, and I knew we were in trouble. The black ink had bled and smeared all over the photo of my earring organizer on the front, top, and side panels. Twenty-five thousand boxes, and you couldn't tell what was supposed to be inside any of them. It was a disaster.

We had only two days before we had to ship out to the stores. I called the printer and they said they'd rerun the boxes and I'd have them in another week. This wasn't going to work. I needed to get them corrected immediately. Production was running. The goods needed to be packaged. The product could not just sit there stacking up in the factory unboxed. The order needed to get out. I jumped in my car and drove three and a half hours to Wisconsin, where the printer was located. Inside, I was frantic; I needed my boxes now.

But I tried to stay calm as I marched into the factory and showed the foreman the ruined boxes. Surely he could see that this was not salable, especially when this was the first time JCPenney had ever done business with me. I then used the same line of reasoning that I did with the manufacturer to explain to him why it was in his best interest to rerun the printrun and re-print my 25,000 boxes. Now. And once again, I begged. This was my first order ever!

The printer wasn't a crook. When I had picked up the phone and explained that he had sent me an unacceptable product, he had agreed to rerun the order. But first he had wanted me to send him a sample overnight, and then he would have put it on press the following week. In other words, he would have gotten to it when it conveniently fit into his production run. But because I drove there right away and was standing in front of him, he had to make me a priority. He could probably see that it would take nothing less than a forklift to move me out of his way, and maybe he even felt sorry for me. He finally agreed to start the print run over immediately. Within twenty-four hours, 25,000 beautiful black boxes were ready to be shipped overnight to the factory so I could meet my deadline.

That's how I operate. At the first hint of a problem, I try to be proactive. I'll jump into my car at a moment's notice for a face-to-face meeting. I'll even get on a plane, if I have to. That's the nature of an entrepreneur. From the very beginning, you have to be willing to do anything within your power to make things happen when needed. This is how you get business done and how you get ahead.

There Are no NOs

Years later, I was faced with another manufacturing conundrum. I had invented a new product called a Fill-A-Bowl. It was a big clear bowl in which you could fill the side walls with different decorative pieces, like candy, beads, or dried flowers. The parts were clear, like my polystyrene organizer, but because of its design, it had an inner smaller bowl and an outer larger bowl that needed to be glued together invisibly. We had to figure out how to successfully adhere the parts without ruining the aesthetics of the product. The only solution would be to use a completely new manufacturing process that would involve a special kind of glue, and press the pieces together so fast and hard they could adhere before the glue dried.

My factory had never done anything like this. Yet as far back as my first earring organizer, every product had always presented a problem, and each time we had put our heads to-gether and figured out how to work around it. I knew we could figure this out—there had to be a way. In this case, however, everyone from the manufacturer's tooling experts, to their engineers, to their

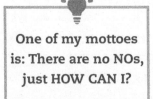

One of my mottoes is: There are no NOs, just HOW CAN I?

factory workers said that what I wanted to do couldn't be done. Finally, I thought, what about a glue expert? So we found one, and sure enough, he figured out what to do.

In the end, the solution was to build an ultraviolet light gluing assembly line, with a conveyor belt that carried the parts at the exact speed for the parts to go under the light and adhere perfectly without ruining the crystal-clear transparence of the bowl.

That Fill-A-Bowl became an overnight sensation, making its way into hundreds of thousands of homes and earning a spot as one of QVC's top five-selling items that year. We also got into Michael's craft stores. For my on-air demo on QVC, I decorated thirty-five different bowls so people could see all the different things you could do with them. I filled them with everything I could think of. It took me weeks. My entire home was strewn with different candies, pastas, beads, and dried flowers. I made a Halloween bowl, a Mardi Gras bowl, and a pasta bowl with macaroni, spirals, and rotini. I made a bowl filled with lavender, rosebuds, and other dried flowers. I made bowl after bowl after bowl. They looked gorgeous, the packaging was gorgeous, and we sold 100,000 Fill-A-Bowls in Michael's in the first six months alone. It was one of the top sellers in all the stores that year, and we were all so glad we'd hung in there and resolved the gluing problem.

LAY THE GROUNDWORK

There is a common theme in these stories: it's not just what you do in the heat of the moment that can save you from disaster, but what you've done in the days before the disaster hits. The groundwork for your business lies just as much in the attention you pay to the people you work with as it does in perfecting the

details of your product. The strength of your relationships will
directly affect how well you're able to get your bus back on track
if things go awry. It's possible you can catch problems and fix
things all by yourself, but it's a lot easier with the goodwill and
cooperation of others.

You must remember that in addition to paying attention to
your direct reports or the people in power, you need to pay attention to all the individuals behind the scenes who make your
business possible. A huge part of my philosophy is to always try
to treat people respectfully and nicely. I see it as homage to my
parents and grandfather, all of whom lived by the same principle.
One of the things I loved and admired most about my grandfather is how he treated everyone the same. He would talk and joke
with a janitor in exactly the same way as he would with a CEO.
He had time for everyone. He instilled in me the philosophy that
it doesn't matter who you are or what you have; what matters is
what kind of person you are.

Kindness and Consideration

The manufacturing plant was located in a Hispanic neighborhood in Chicago. Many of the employees who worked there
didn't speak English well. Fortunately, I spoke passable Spanish.
The plant ran twenty-four hours a day. I would come in almost
every day, and often in the evenings, too.

Sometimes we would get an order that would overwhelm the
factory and we would not be able to make the product as quickly
as the store wanted. Sometimes there might be an outbreak of
colds or flu, during which the fac-
tory would lose a handful of employees per shift. We were lucky
that the product was doing so well
on QVC, but deadlines could be so

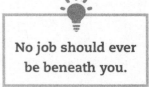

**No job should ever
be beneath you.**

tight it meant that sometimes there wouldn't be time for the factory workers to shrink-wrap everything to get the product out as urgently as needed. When these situations occurred, I found it was helpful if I came in to help out, lend a hand. So Dan and I would come in at midnight and walk around and around the pallets with what amounted to a tremendous roll of Saran Wrap. God bless Dan; he was always there by my side to help when I needed it. Once we shrink-wrapped three hundred pallets in a weekend just by ourselves.

A factory floor is no picnic. At this one, the hot injection-molding presses were located on the first floor and generated a lot of heat; and heat rises, as we all know. The factory was not air-conditioned. In the summer, on particularly hot days, the factory could get close to one hundred degrees on the second floor, where the assembly line to package my product was located. Chicago summers can be hot, so everyone was dripping with sweat, working hard, checking details, trimming edges, and packing product. It was super uncomfortable, but unbelievably, we would all get used to it.

I felt bad because it was so hot. I brought in fans to help cool the space, and I tried to have lots of ice-cold drinks and special treats available to make the heat more bearable. I wish the factory could have been air-conditioned, but as I said earlier, it was almost a hundred years old. The women who worked so hard on my product during those hot days were amazing. They touched my heart and soul. I love them to this day. We were on the journey together.

One of the most touching by-products of doing what little I could to make these women's workdays more pleasant was that they became protective of me. Every now and then, I'd get a phone call in the middle of the night, and in Spanish, someone who was working the night shift would say, "Hola,

Lori," and then tell me there was a quality issue with what they were packing. They'd tell me to come in the next day, ask to do a surprise inspection, and look for boxes with a line drawn on them. Those were the boxes I should open. I was so moved that they cared enough about me that they would take the risk of contacting me because they wanted to make sure I was getting good product. They trusted that I would never betray them.

It was a two-way street—I cared about them, and they cared about me. Sure enough, when I'd do an inspection the next morning and open a box with a line drawn on it, inside would be organizers with slight scratches or that had something else wrong with them. Immediately, the foreman and factory owners would apologize for the oversight and promise to redo the order. I never stopped letting the factory workers know how grateful I was for the way they looked out for me.

To this day I'll never forget the work ethic of a night foreman named Andy, who worked the second shift at the factory. He looked like Popeye. He had served in the navy and wore a crew cut. His arms were covered in tattoos and he rolled his cigarettes up in his shirtsleeve. His hands were workman's hands— rough, covered in oil and grease. He was a salt-of-the-earth kind of guy, and one of the nicest, most caring people who worked at the factory. He often worked fixing the injection-molding presses, which are enormous machines that clamp together with tons of force while pushing molten plastic into the nooks and crannies of the mold. They're hot and unwieldy, and they can have sharp metal pieces.

One night I saw Andy fixing one of the machines and I stopped to say hello. All of a sudden he let out a yell, and when he pulled his hand out of the machine, blood went flying. I started hunting for a clean rag to use as a tourniquet and shrieked, "We have to get you to the ER!" But he replied, "Nah. I can't leave." Ignoring him, crazy with panic, I kept talking while hunting for a tourniquet. It was a bad gash.

"Andy, you're BLEEDING! You're gushing all over . . . I can't find a rag . . . ."

As I started to think I'd have to rip up my own shirt, he said calmly, "I'll be fine," pulled out a blowtorch, and cauterized his own hand. I stopped only long enough to pull in another huge gulp of air and then started screaming again,

"My God, now you're BURNED! We have to get you to the hospital! Now!"

And he looked at me with the faintest grin and drawled, "Nah, I do it all the time. Plus I can't leave my team all alone. I gotta look out for them."

Andy died several years ago, but often when I look back and think about his dedication and devotion, and about all the teams we had in the early days, I'm overwhelmed by the fabulous working spirit of these individuals whom I came to know and love.

Face Issues Head-on

You've got to be kind, and considerate, and appreciative, but you've also got to be tough in this business. I try to promote a team-oriented culture, and even a sense of family, at every

> It's always important to call out any problems or issues. Don't be afraid to speak up and make sure things are done right.

level in my business, but I try not to let my personal feelings cloud my judgment when it comes to making decisions in the best interest of my company or my products. Once, after yet another surprise inspection revealed imperfect product getting ready to be shipped out to retailers, I called a meeting with one of the factory owners. We decided to have it on the loading dock.

I arrived first. I had already thought about the best way to address what was becoming an increasing problem of bad product knowingly being packed into boxes, but I didn't want to alienate him. I looked up and saw the owner plus his brother and his son approaching me. The way they were walking reminded me of gunslingers approaching the sheriff for a showdown in the town square. As they approached, I said jokingly, "Wow, I didn't know there would be three of you! Here come the Hauser men to beat up on me." And one of them, whom I liked a lot, and who became a good friend, turned to the other two and said jokingly, "We're going to need more men." They knew they weren't going to be able to get away with the status quo anymore.

THERE IS ALWAYS A WAY

> **Put things in perspective, no matter what the crisis, and then move on.**

When you're an entrepreneur, you just can't let anything or anyone get in your way, no matter how dire the situation. You can almost always find a solution if you try hard enough. And if you've laid the right groundwork, on those rare occasions when you can't find a solution, you'll find that the consequences are usually far less severe than you feared they'd be.

Let's say a container full of goods coming in for the holiday season gets waterlogged and ruined. That's not something you can fix. You've got three thousand soggy units, and there aren't enough hair dryers or fans in the world to dry them out. Gone is gone. But you've been wise enough to get insurance, right? So you're covered. So then what's the worst thing? You lose sales. That's a big deal, but your buyer will know it's not your fault. You may not get holiday placement—sales results are key. But if you've built a good relationship with your buyer, you hope they will get you back on the shelves with your next order. You're more likely to get a second chance than if you don't have a good relationship. You've suffered a setback, yes, but you can work to change things around tomorrow.

DRIVING THE BUSINESS TO-DO LIST:

❑ When problems occur, think out of the box. There is *always* a solution.

❑ Make the people you work with feel valued and part of a team.

❑ Show your appreciation for what they do.

❑ If you make special requests, or need something in a rush, explain why so people understand why it's important.

10

BEYOND BRICK AND MORTAR

"There is no elevator to success; you have to take the stairs."

—AUTHOR UNKNOWN

INVENTORS TODAY ARE SO LUCKY. THROUGHOUT MOST OF THE nineteenth and twentieth centuries, the only way to sell your new product, unless you went door to door, was through brick-and-mortar stores or mail-order catalogs. In the last two decades, however, our options have mushroomed, allowing us to sell from the old stand-bys, as well as through TV, our own websites, online retailers, and social commerce sites. Interestingly, all of this e-commerce, which some might have predicted would weaken direct response marketing channels like television home shopping networks the way Amazon decimated bookstores, has instead only served to increase their power, prestige, and sales reach.

Though all the above selling venues should play a role in your selling strategy, in my opinion there is simply no better selling medium for a new inventor than a shopping channel like

QVC. A few minutes on QVC can open up a whole world of retail opportunities. In addition, it puts you in the same company as brands like Apple, Nikon, Bose, and Wii for electronics; Philosophy, Clinique, and L'Occitane for makeup; and Calvin Klein, Lucky Brand, and Dooney & Bourke for fashion, among thousands of others. Every big brand wants to be on QVC. It's king. It's an $8.5 billion retailer that shipped more than 166 million products in 2012 across its global markets. Its viewing audience is comparable in scale to major networks like Lifetime, Bravo, and A&E, and it ranks no.2 in mobile commerce among multicategory retailers, second only to Amazon.

WHY TELEVISION STILL MATTERS IN THE INTERNET AGE

I made my career on TV because I happened to invent highly demonstrable products, so that's where I knew I would see my biggest success. There's nowhere else I know of where you can sell thousands of units within minutes (their first time on QVC, the inventors of FiberFix, one of my *Shark Tank* deals, sold 16,000 units in ten minutes, the equivalent of $300,000 at retail). As discussed in Chapter 2, demonstrable products are items that can be physically demonstrated in front of consumers so they can immediately witness and experience the product's features, benefits, and problem-solving capabilities.

It's all about the visuals. A lamp is not demonstrable—unless it can adjust its brightness according to the amount of natural light coming into a room. A picture frame just hangs there, inanimate. But a frame that shows over a hundred photos with the press of a button, one flipping to the next to the next, is demonstrable and could possibly sell well on television. Even ordinary objects that don't usually bear a second thought can become demonstrable. For instance, everyone thinks they know what a vacuum cleaner does, until they watch one pick up glass, nails, sand, and even bowling balls. Suddenly, the consumer becomes aware that all vacuum cleaners are not the same.

With a demonstrable product, the consumer can see physical proof that one item is better than another. Jewelry is an example of something that is not demonstrable, yet it sells really well on TV because people can decide instantly whether or not they like it; and TV shopping channels bring jewelry to the consumer in an affordable, informative, and fun way. It's an impulse buy. Television allows consumers to understand products in a way that even the best packaging displayed on a retail shelf cannot.

Aside from demonstrability, the questions you'd ask to determine whether you product is right for TV are similar to the ones you'd ask of any other product you wanted to sell:

- Is it unique?
- Is there a need for it?
- Is it a good price point?
- Have you done research that indicates the market wants it?
- Is it affordable? Typically, for a product to sell on a TV shopping channel, the cost has to be at least $14.00 or more to the consumer, because once you factor in the cost of shipping you don't want the consumer to pay more for shipping and handling than they do for the product. So QVC, for example, does not sell products for under $14.00, and it's why inexpensive items under $10.00 are usually sold in a set of two or three on shopping channels.
- Is it a manageable size? Your product can't be too massive because it needs to be something that can easily ship or for which people would be willing to

pay shipping and handling. The larger and heavier
the item, the higher the shipping and handling costs.

If your product meets all of these criteria, you probably have
the makings of a successful television sales item.

WHO BUYS FROM TELEVISION SHOPPING NETWORKS?

It is not primarily for grandmothers, as Kevin O'Leary once
sniped on *Shark Tank*. I get along great with Kevin, but as I joked
right after he said it, that day his comment made me want to
pull out my driver and hit his bald, white, dimply head a hundred
yards away from me. Here's how badly misinformed Kevin is.

Television shopping networks do appeal to a highly female
demographic, but so do most retail sellers: women are the main
buyers in all consumer categories except electronics. However,
men shop on television, too. At QVC, 15 percent of customers
are men. Twenty-three percent of customers are 25 to 44-year-old
women; 48 percent are 45 to 64 years old.

The audience includes shoppers from every socioeconomic
demographic. Eighty-eight percent are homeowners with an
average net worth of $249,000; a significant number live in the
tony 90210 California zip code. Once QVC wanted to reward all
the people who spent $500,000 a year or more with the channel
by inviting them to a special event. As the attendees streamed
through the doors of the studio, it was enlightening to see what
a diverse group they actually were. They represented the typical customers you'd see walking down the street in any major
city—all ages, all ethnicities, moms with daughters, husbands
and wives.

At one time, people might have been reluctant to admit
that they shopped on television, but like Internet dating, it has

gone mainstream, and is considered a welcome convenience in our busy, busy lives. Most if not all of the networks have mobile apps that allow consumers to watch the shows and shop on their digital devices. *Shark Tank*, too, has added to people's awareness of the medium, not just because I'm on it but also because entrepreneurs know the extreme value of getting on QVC. Give an entrepreneur a shot at QVC, which is by far the largest of the TV shopping networks (HSN and ShopHQ, previously ShopNBC, are second and third, respectively), and they act like you've given them the moon.

The reason entrepreneurs love television shopping networks is that they offer inventors a number of advantages:

- *Tremendous reach.* The audience is massive—both QVC and HSN command an audience in slightly fewer than one hundred million U.S. homes.
- *Instant sales.* If your product is right for the medium, meaning it is highly demonstrable and desired, you have the potential to sell literally thousands of units in minutes. A typical sell on QVC lasts between six and eight minutes. That represents a lot of units sold in an extremely short amount of time.
- *Free marketing and advertising.* Your presentation can greatly increase your consumer's familiarity with your brand. Television sales don't just sell your product on TV; they help you sell it everywhere else.
- *Free market research.* In retail stores, you could wait months to find out whether consumers want your product and if it will sell well. When you present on television, however, you know immediately whether your product is a hero or a zero.

- *Instant customer feedback.* It's so exciting and
  gratifying to see the big numbers sold. You can
  see the ticker on-screen going from a hundred to a
  thousand to five thousand in just minutes. The best,
  of course, is seeing the sold-out sign come up. If
  you're selling good numbers, it's a great gauge of how
  people feel about your product.

After airing on a TV shopping channel, some entrepreneurs see explosive sales spikes both online and in-store as well—sometimes as high as 30 percent. When you look at a product on a retail shelf, you don't know half of what it does until you can take it home and try it yourself. The packaging does all the talking. But on a television sales show, your product has a voice.

When I demonstrate my no-mess cooking utensils, I can show home cooks how they never need to mess up their counters by setting dirty utensils on them or using a dish as a spoon rest, just by stirring and hanging my utensil on the side of the pot. Viewers can watch me close the lid over the utensils, how I can touch the handles and not get burned because they are silicone coated, and how they are great as cooking utensils and serving utensils, too. I can also try the same experiment with a competitor's cooking utensil, and show what I call the submarine spoon that dives under the surface when you set it alongside the rim. Viewers can see for themselves the difference, and why my product is better. I can dramatize the problem, and show you the solutions.

You can't get the same perspective when you see cooking utensils dangling from a cardboard hangtag in a store. The demonstration makes the item for sale seem alluring and seductive. The product looks wonderful, you're showing off its usefulness, and how much you enjoy using it, and suddenly, the consumers just have to try it for themselves. And if you produce good quality products, they'll be glad they did.

As for the instantaneous feedback, television retailers often let you speak directly to your consumers while you're selling. QVC, for example, will often put up a testimonial phone number on the screen to give people a chance to call in and express their opinions about a brand or product. Customers call in to order and are asked to speak on air, or they can ask to do it. I love talking to my customers live! In addition, customers can post comments and reviews online for you to review and respond to. With so many ways for customers to offer their opinions, it doesn't take long to know whether your product is a hero.

HOW TO GET ON THE AIR

Something not many people know is that I was actually rejected by QVC the first time I tried to sell my product there. I became familiar with the channel because my mother had started watching it after hurting her back and shopping had become difficult for her. She loved how easy it was to pick up the phone, place your order, and see your items show up on your doorstep a few days later. She was hooked, and I was amazed at how engrossing it was.

Right after I created my first product, I realized how highly demonstrable it was, and I knew it would be perfect for TV sales. So even as I successfully stalked retailers with my redial button, landing a contract with JCPenney and eventually Marshall Fields, among other retailers, I made the television channels my other main goal. I sent QVC a sample of my product. They promptly returned it to me with a "No, thank you." It's somewhat easier to get on now, but back then, once you were turned away, that was it. The wall was virtually impenetrable. I was disappointed, but there were other fish in the sea. I decided to set my sights on the Home Shopping Network, as HSN was then called.

Once again, I spent weeks hitting the redial button, trying to reach the Home Shopping Network buyer's office in Tampa. Finally, one evening right before 5 p.m., a woman picked up the phone. I blurted out my quick line about my revolutionary new product as fast as I could, and then told her that I was going to be in Tampa, and I would love to introduce myself in person (as usual, I did not have a ticket to Tampa, but if she said she'd meet me, the very next call I made was going to be to the airlines). That's when the woman interrupted me. "Let me stop you," she said. "I'm only going to be the buyer two more weeks. I'm moving to Chicago, so I really won't be able to help you."

Famous last words. I replied, "Funny coincidence, I'm from Chicago. If there's anything you need or want, or any information I can give you about Chicago to get you set up, I'd be happy to help. Would you please just pass me on to whoever is the next buyer?"

And she said, "You know, I actually could use some help. Sure."

And that's how I got my big break on television. I flew down to meet the new buyer, a woman named Laurie Meyer, and showed her my earring organizer. Next thing I knew, she had ordered three thousand units and told me to be ready to go on the air in six weeks. My product was made in the United States, and injection-molded manufacturers typically make thousands of units a week, so I could place an order and get it to their warehouse right away. That's another huge benefit of making a product in the United States—you don't need the thirty-five to forty-five days on the water, through the port, and trucking to a warehouse the way products made overseas do.

PITCHING FOR TV BUYERS

Which shopping networks should you aim for? Shopping networks generally carry similar types of items—home goods, cosmetics, jewelry, electronics, and apparel—though brands and price points vary. QVC is known for showing a wide variety of products in quick succession, more than a thousand per week; HSN keeps products on the air for longer periods of time. Not everyone is going to open the door for you, especially if you have only one item to sell. The TV shopping channels want the next big thing! It helps if you are an entrepreneur who knows the ropes, but that doesn't mean an inventor with one terrific product can't get a spot on any of these channels. It just means that there is a bigger learning curve and it will be more of a challenge than if you had several items to offer. The channels seem to be moving toward opening up more to new entrepreneurs than before, based on the establishment of initiatives like QVC's Sprouts program, which allows viewers to vote on which new inventions will get a shot on the air.

You pitch differently to a television buyer than to a buyer for a brick-and-mortar store. A good product is a good product; they're both going to want it. But there are considerations a brick-and-mortar store buyer must think about that a television buyer does not. Packaging, for example. In a brick-and-mortar setting, it's understood that your packaging is going to do a lot of your selling for you. It's also going to determine to a degree whether the item is easy for the store to stock and display. Size matters a lot. Shape matters. Retailers have space considerations that television channels do not.

I sell a fun and hugely popular item called CordaRoy's Beanbag Bed. It was one of my *Shark Tank* deals. It's a comfy beanbag that unzips and turns into a plush full-size bed! It's packaged in a large box, though, so when we wanted to sell it to retailers, we had to figure out ahead of time how to address their inevitable concern about how they were going to store and display such a big piece. Our solution was to suggest they display one beanbag bed but pack the colorful slipcovers separately in little hanging bags. That way people could see the shape and size of the bed, and choose from an array of colors, but the store didn't have to stock a large box for every color, which would take up too much shelf and warehouse space. This goes back to thinking ahead when you are pitching and trying to address every question a buyer could possibly have, anticipating any problem, and showing that you have a solution ready.

When you're pitching to a buyer for a TV shopping channel, be passionate, show your product come to life, and be as appealing as you hope your product will be. TV sales are a visual medium, so make sure the buyer falls in love with you and your product. For example, the beanbag is an easy pitch. "First, it's a beanbag, and then you unzip the outer cover and it transforms into a bed! Give your guests a comfortable place to rest when they arrive without having to store a large bulky air mattress in an overstuffed closet when they leave. It's fun and practical furniture that solves a problem." And the size of the product wasn't an issue. QVC (and HSN) ships a large percentage of what they sell, but some items, especially large ones or food, are drop-shipped directly from the supplier's own warehouse or factory.

Passion and enthusiasm are infectious. People always tell me that I come across so passionately about my products. I genuinely love them, and it shows. *You have to be genuine.* If I don't like it, I'm not going to sell it. Some inventors do go on and sell their products, but not everybody is comfortable on TV or wants to be on TV. A lot of the people who sell products on TV are called "on-air demonstrators." They did not create the product, but they are hired by the company to be the pitch person or demonstrator on air. You'll see them more often than an inventor selling his or her product. That's because more large companies and brands make products than do individual inventors.

Consider yourself lucky to get in where you can, and do your very best to make your time on the air so successful that the network can't wait to invite you back. That's how you make more opportunities happen. In fact, that's how I finally got onto QVC. Once I started successfully selling on Home Shopping Network, I called QVC UK in London, and told them that I had this great product that was selling like gangbusters on the Home Shopping Network in the United States. I gave them my sales numbers and sent them a sample, and they agreed to let me on the air.

So I flew to London and sold my earring organizer on QVC UK, where it sold out. Then I called the shopping channel in Canada and followed the same script. They let me on the air, and it sold out. By then I had started developing more products, and within months I was selling all of them in the United States, the UK, and Canada. I kept rolling over the money, putting it back into the business so I could keep making new products. The pressure was intense. On TV, you're only as good as your last performance, and it was nerve-wracking because I never knew whether I'd meet with the same sales the next time I walked out in front of the cameras. I proceeded with confidence, but I never took anything for granted, because things can always change. Fortunately for me, when they did, it was decidedly in my favor.

I was extremely happy working with Home Shopping Network and felt extreme gratitude and loyalty to the buyer who had made my career there possible. But then she was moved to become the buyer of accessories, and we no longer worked together. Her replacement took a long time to get settled in and didn't return my calls or reach out to me. This is not unusual. Buyers are busy. She was getting familiar with a new position and I just had a few SKUs, so I probably was not considered very important. But I had no idea when I was going to get another purchase order, if ever. I hung in there for at least three months, but then I decided I couldn't stay there in limbo forever.

So I called Laurie, my original Home Shopping Network buyer, and asked if she would be upset if I tried to sell to QVC. She told me that she understood my position and that I should do what was best for my business. I called my QVC UK buyer and told her I'd like to go on QVC USA, and could she make the necessary introductions? She did, and the buyer ordered three thousand units and scheduled an air date. I was terrified, because I was suddenly faced with a big choice: stay with Home Shopping Network where I knew the ropes and felt I could continue to enjoy success (assuming the buyer there ever got back to me), or try selling on another channel and risk falling flat on my face and losing everything. That's because as soon as Home Shopping Network knew that I had sold on QVC, they would terminate my product there.

These channels are very competitive, and it is not often that you would sell on both at the same time. Also, there are better and worse time slots and days of the week, and there was no way to predict which ones the QVC USA buyer would give me. What if I tanked? In TV sales, if you don't sell well you rarely get another chance to present. The bottom line in airtime is money, and you need to do the dollars per minute required for your assigned time slot to stay on air and be reordered. Fortunately, when I went on QVC, my product sold out. Funny, though. Within minutes of going off the air my phone rang. It was the director of my product category at HSN, who must have just seen or heard that I was selling on QVC. And she was NOT happy. I formally switched and began selling exclusively on QVC. Sixteen years later, I'm still there.

HOW TO SELL SUCCESSFULLY ON TV

I was completely unprepared for my first performance ever on the air, for the Home Shopping Network, and it was not quite what I expected. I thought I'd arrive at the studio and get a crash course on television sales, maybe even a dry run. No such luck. Nowadays networks prep presenters and there's an on-air guest class, but at that time they just threw you on the air. Dan accompanied me to Florida, and as soon as we arrived at HSN, they sent us to the green room, where Billy Mays of OxiClean fame was also waiting to go on air. I sat down and asked him what I was supposed to do, and he said, "Just go out there and demo it. It's no different from showing it to a friend."

Next thing I knew, an assistant called my name, escorted me to the set, and clipped a mic on me. Luckily, I was not standing there all by myself. Next to me stood a lovely woman named Chris Scanlin, who, right before the cameras started rolling, whispered reassuringly, "Don't worry! This is a really cool product." Then she went on to do 80 percent of the talking. Thank goodness for that, because I wasn't sure what to do or how it all worked. She asked me so many questions about the organizer that it was almost like an interview.

Recently I looked back at the video, and it's so funny—how I just stood there barely touching my earring organizer, which is hilarious, because if there's one thing I'm known for, it's constantly moving and demonstrating my product. As I stood there, thoughts were running through my mind: *Oh, my God, I'm not sure what happens next . . . they just threw me out here—what do I do??* Then Chris looked over at me with a big smile and informed me that we just sold out. It was over in a flash.

We had just sold three thousand units in eight minutes. Not only that, we actually oversold by 30 percent. That was a big deal! I was stunned, but so incredibly happy. This was a sign we had made it. The product was going to be a success. Next thing I knew, my buyer was asking me how fast we could get more product and was scheduling me for another airing before Christmas. I headed straight to my factory, made more product, and got right back down to Florida as soon as possible. I made regular appearances every four to six weeks for a year. And as anyone who watches me on TV today can tell, I got more comfortable and a lot better at talking about and demonstrating my product. Now it's second nature.

I think about that moment—what a big deal it was to Dan and me, how nervous I was, how excited I was, and how thrilling it was when I sold out. Every time I bring one of my new entrepreneurs' products on to QVC, I try my best to make sure they're not nervous or worried, and that we've covered everything we need to ensure the product's success. I want them to experience what it feels like to see the "sold out" sign come up!

Trying to beat me out of a deal, Kevin O'Leary once told a *Shark Tank* contestant that "TV ladies" are a dime a dozen. That's like saying that any investment banker can get the same results as Kevin. No, to stay alive and relevant on television takes a tremendous amount of hard work, sharp instincts, and guts. There's an art to knowing your business inside out. Not every airing is a hit. There are so many factors involved that are completely out of your control, such as what time of day you will air, what day of the week, and so on. But then knowing how to navigate the system, knowing how to present a product on TV, knowing all the minutiae of TV sales is something I've been learning my entire career.

First, you have to know what's a good product. Next, you have to know what's right for TV. Then, there are the best demo techniques, the perfect price points, and navigating your way through the ins and outs of the business. There are so many facets to selling successfully on a TV shopping channel. I've seen so many vendors and representatives come and go. Even just to get on QVC your product has to move through their quality assurance department, pass their eleven-point drop test, be compliant with all their rules and regulations—and that's just to be able to get a purchase order. Then you have to be successful. The majority of products last less than a few years on QVC. So believe me, getting on TV and staying on TV is a lot harder than it looks. Kevin and some of the other sharks know this, because their products have been on QVC and then disappeared.

> As many times as somebody may hit pay dirt, somebody else will fall in the mud. There's never a guarantee.

To sell successfully on television, you must do the following:

Find the Right Formula

The truth is, just getting on TV is often the easy part. No item is ever a shoo-in, even those sold by celebrity endorsers; the customers are far savvier than to buy a product just because it bears the name of a famous person. You have to make magic happen, and you have to have a great product if you're going to get asked back. Successful television retail requires no less than an ideal combination of great demonstrable product sold in the perfect way by the right person at the right time on the right day of the week. The formula really is that precise.

Earn Your Dollars per Minute

To get a reorder and a new airing, you have to earn at minimum whatever number of dollars per minute have been set for that day of the week in that time slot, and for that time of year. For example, an item sold on Monday at 3 p.m. might be required to sell $5,000 per minute. If you don't reach that goal, you might not be reordered and your product could be returned to you. Brick-and-mortar stores will give you a longer chance to find your audience; your product can live forever on your website. But on TV, the first time your sales don't keep up with expectations, you're probably done, because QVC has to find another product that will.

Of course, if you exceed your goal—say, you sell $6,000 or $7,000 per minute—you'll quickly get a reorder and a new airing. But you have to sustain that number each time you appear. If you start to slow down, it will appear it has had its day, and the channel may discontinue selling the item. It is probably more difficult to succeed in television sales than in any other sales medium. On the flip side, if you do succeed, it can be huge! You can literally sell hundreds of thousands of dollars in minutes. You might be able sell the same number of units and earn the same amount of money in a retail store if it is a chain with a large number of stores, but you'll still have to do it over a much longer period of time.

Time Your Product Right

Timing is extremely important in TV sales. You can kill a great product if you launch it at the wrong time or during the wrong season. I should know; I did it. I had created a 22-piece centerpiece collection that could be configured in all kinds of ways to hold flowers, floating candles, taper candles, shrimp, nuts, dips, or whatever struck your imagination. It did everything but cook your meal for you. QVC had selected it as one of my first "Today's Special Value" items. The product was glamorous and beautiful, and an amazing price. I knew it would be a perfect pre-holiday sales item. But my buyers at QVC needed a pre-Mother's Day TSV and needed someone to fill it. Although I felt it was a pre-Christmas item, I went along. At this early time in my career I'd only been lucky enough to get a few "Today's Special Values," so I wasn't going to pass up the opportunity. It turned into one of my biggest failures.

Unfortunately, once something doesn't work on air, the TV networks lose interest in it, and you have to work incredibly hard to get them to let you try again. Fortunately, though some product was returned to me, QVC still had some left in stock that they needed to sell. The network let me put the centerpiece back on the air during the pre-holiday season, where it did great. But by then none of us had the enthusiasm we should have had for the product and once it sold out, it was never to be seen again.

Another time, I went on the air just as President Bill Clinton held a press conference and delivered his infamous statement, "I did not have sexual relations with that woman." No one was watching QVC that day, and my product hardly sold at all. It just goes to show how unpredictable the television retail environment can be. I remember walking out of the studio thinking, "I'm dead." But I did get a second chance.

Another time I had a "Today's Special Value" that wound up being on the same day as the last twenty-four hours of the countdown to the Iraq War. Everybody's eyes were glued to CNN, not QVC. The programming was set; there was nothing I could do. As you can imagine, that was a hell of bad day.

Be Prepared for Anything!

Live TV can set you up for all kinds of hilarious situations. The trick is to stay on your toes and roll with it. I've had a liter bottle of seltzer water explode in my face; an electric can opener that wouldn't work; I've burned my hand on a molten hot butane lighter. And during the only blackout in QVC history, I was selling live on air. As luck would have it, I was selling magical floating water candles. They came in quite handy that day.

Another time I went to Dusseldorf to sell on QVC Germany. I got to the studio and I saw the name of the show I was going to be on, called *The Schmuck Galerie*. Oh, my God! It turns out the German word for jewelry is "schmuck." Then I saw on the screen that the name of the product is the "Ohrring-Aufbewahrungs-system." I thought that was hilarious. That first appearance on QVC Germany went well, and we were invited back with other products, eventually getting a "Today's Special Value" for my full-length mirror jewelry cabinet.

Everyone on the program wears an earpiece so we can hear the callers, but since I don't speak a word of German, when I'm selling on QVC Germany I wear two earpieces when I'm live on air—one in one ear for the callers, and one in the other ear for the translator who tells me in English what the callers or host is saying. So, one time, I was kicking off a "Today's Special Value" at midnight; there's a huge amount of money on the line. I start to sell, and in one ear I hear German. Then I hear the translator's voice in my other ear . . . in *German*. I have no idea what anyone is saying. For fourteen excruciatingly long minutes, I winged it. There was no way to let anyone know something was wrong. I kept talking in English: "This mirror jewelry cabinet is fabulous because you store 350 pieces and it all hangs! And isn't it fabulous—it has an antitarnish lining!" I'm sure the audience and everyone in the studio thought I was nuts, for surely I wasn't responding correctly to anything the host was saying.

Amazingly, the product sold. That just goes to show you how much television retail relies on the demonstrability of a product. What you say is extremely important, but what you do on the air is almost more so.

Keep Things Exciting

An important aspect about TV is that you have to keep things fresh and new. People will get bored if every time they tune in, the channel is always selling the same ten items. So once you've built momentum, get ready to mix things up—not with your demonstration, but with your product itself. Maybe you could add features or offer a better deal. My line of jewelry organizers have been on QVC for sixteen years, and they're still going strong as ever because I tweak them to keep them fresh, even as I preserve everything that has made them such classics.

I did the same thing with my no-mess cooking utensils that hung on the side of the pot so they wouldn't mess up kitchen countertops. The set included a stirring spoon, a slotted spoon, a fat gravy separator, and a ladle. After two years, however, we could see sales starting to slip a little. So what did we do? We made the heads larger, and we developed a pasta fork and a spatula. Everyone loved them and started requesting a nonstick version. And then we went back to the original set of four and made them in the larger size, but kept them at their original price. In this way, we were able to maintain the concept that everyone loved and was doing great for us, while making the product feel new.

You have to constantly think and be creative. Adding colors to a product is often a great move for TV. If the home cook who loves red accents in her kitchen suddenly sees that those cool

THE RULES OF SELLING ON A HOME SHOPPING CHANNEL:

1. *No overselling.* That means no hard pushing. An info-mercial sell is often exaggerated. They will show videos of people shaking their heads in dismay over whatever problem the product being sold is supposed to solve. It always looks stilted and fake. QVC promotes a backyard fence attitude of selling. Though we do film video footage, it is simply to show the item in action in its natural environment, and not in dramatizations. When pitching your product on a home shopping channel, you should always sound like you're just hanging out at home explaining to a friend or neighbor why you're passionate about your product.

2. *No pressure.* Infomercials usually come with calls to action. "Pick up the phone NOW and you'll get two, plus a carrying case!" On QVC, there are no throw-ins or add-ons if you dial in. You get whatever is advertised. The only thing that might influence a consumer to buy sooner rather than later are the numbers appearing on the screen announcing how many items have sold and how many are left.

3. *Talking points.* Make sure to get out your talking points and demo the benefits and features you planned.

4. *Video.* Use videos to supplement your demo. Before and after videos are particularly useful for demonstrating your product's problem solving capabilities.

5. *Clean.* No swearing if you ever want to be invited back on air.

no-mess cooking utensils that used to be available only in black are now available in red, you have a good chance of finally making that sale. Playing with colors and expanded product lines reveals yet another advantage to television: brick-and-mortar retailers may not have the space to keep that many colors and SKUs, whereas on TV you can show as many as you like.

CLEVER AND UNIQUE CREATIONS

For two years I'd come on the air for the usual seven or eight minutes given all products on QVC. All along, however, I had my eye on the prize: my own hour-long show. There are two types of shows—branded and generic. *Generic* shows represent all types of different products from different companies. *Branded* shows represent several products, but they are all from the same brand. There might be a Dooney & Bourke hour or a Philosophy hour.

My goal was a Lori Greiner hour. I was told that to qualify, I would have to invent seven to nine items that were consistently successful every time they went on the air. At QVC, as I've shared, a successful product is defined as one that earns all the dollars per minute for that hour required for a reorder. With every new invention, I'd pray that it would work well enough to get me a little closer to my goal of one day getting my own show. If you sell on QVC you're constantly meeting with your buyers, and as we would talk about the products and strategize, I was always hoping that eventually we'd see that I had enough products earning enough sales to get me that special hour. But it wasn't just about the numbers; I also needed to establish that I was a big enough brand that could carry an hour-long show.

In my third year, I got it. It's called "Clever and Unique Creations by Lori Greiner," and I still have it to this day, multiple times each month. For me, selling in that hour was so much more fun than the eight minutes I was accustomed to. It also proved a great way to build my brand even more. A show makes you a destination, giving your customers a dedicated place to find you and your products. In addition, it ensures that you can get a lot of feedback from your customers, which is wonderful because then you can make sure to take their needs and wants into account as you create more products. I adore the QVC followers and customers. I would not be where I am today without them and their support and dedication. They have made what I do for a living truly gratifying.

It was around the time that I got my own show that my travel schedule meant I was away from home almost more than I was home. Dan, a CPA, had been doing my accounting all along, but when the traveling became too much, he quit his job and joined me full time as VP so that we could spend all our time together. The business had grown so much that we were financially secure enough to no longer worry about losing his income. The business was getting exciting and he wanted to be a part of it with me. I was president, he became vice president. In addition to taking care of the books, he also took over the shipping and back-end operations. I continued to handle the product creation, manufacturing, selling, marketing, all legal, and running and driving the company. We couldn't be happier; we play to each other's strengths.

BEHIND THE SCENES

When the QVC audience tunes in to see you and your product, they would probably never guess how much planning and hard work went into getting ready for that show during the months, days, and even the hours just before you appeared on air. It's something that new entrepreneurs always find surprising, too.

For example, a typical day for me on QVC might start at 8 or 9 a.m. if I'm lucky—sometimes I can have several of my hour shows within a 24-hour period (a "Today's Special Value" is the toughest schedule, representing about 36 hours of no sleep). Unfortunately, you can't just set the show up and leave it until your next airing, because other people are using the studio. It takes us three to four hours to set up for each show, so we're going to be working hard all day.

QVC offers all on-air guests a stylist to do their hair and makeup, but I do my own at home because I'd rather use the extra time to help my team set up and talk with the host and the QVC production team. Typically I'm always rushing to get dressed. I push everything to the last minute. In fact, my team has taken to telling me that I need to be somewhere a half hour earlier than I really do so as to make sure I'm out the door when they want me to be.

I consider many things when picking out my outfits—no wild patterns, no crazy color combinations, no supershort skirts, no jeans, and so on, per QVC guidelines. I try to be attractive and stylish, but not distracting. I'm representing my brand—the main event is the product.

If I'm going to be presenting a product that I haven't done very frequently, or that's relatively new, I often watch a recording of the last time I presented it on air to see what I liked in the sell, what worked or didn't work, and what I think I could do better. It's a good refresher. (I've sold some products so many times I could sell them in my sleep!)

The decision about what I am going to sell today was made months ago. I'll have a general overview for the quarter, and then as we get closer to the shows, QVC's buying and planning team will tell us what's going to be in each hour. So then I know which six to seven items to prepare for. A combination of the new and the existing bestsellers make up each hour show.

We plan weeks ahead of time for how we are going to demo the brand-new products. I used to do it all myself; now I'm lucky and I get a lot of help from Coop, my director of marketing, broadcasting, and social media. I usually start out with a vision in my head of how the demo should go. However, there are two essential elements you always need to emphasize:

1. Your product's features

2. Your product's benefits

You'll hear those two words discussed all the time at QVC. Your product's *features* are all the things it is and does. Customers need to be able to see those to know if the product is something that might be useful and whether it is appealing and to their taste. But equally important are the *benefits* of those features. Why does someone need this product? It will make her or him more organized. It is more convenient. It will clean the home more thoroughly. Whatever you are selling, you have to continually point out how the features and benefits of your product will make a consumer's life better.

Aside from the product's features and benefits, we put together all kinds of visuals to help explain why the product is great. Products we've sold before are propped and stored in a warehouse, but the new ones need a lot of planning. Several weeks before the show, my team and I select which props will help us convey on air everything the product can do. How will we demo this? How will we demo that?

We will also film support videos a few months ahead of time.

You'll see these lifestyle support videos run two or three times during the live on-air sell. Everybody makes them. A video can escalate your sales by as much as 20 percent, if not more. They help people see the product in action in the right environment, not just in a studio. Take, for example, my favorite luggage, my deluxe weekender bag, which I designed for myself. The lid is a flap into which you can snap a toiletry bag; and when you open the bag up, you can hook the flap onto the telescoping handle so you can see all of your toiletries and cosmetics. It's got a lot of neat, patented benefits and features other bags don't have.

In the studio, I can show how it unzips to reveal the toiletry case snapped inside the lid. But it also has 360 degree turning wheels and fit into a plane's overhead compartment. You can see some of this in the on-air demonstration, but some of the benefits can't be demonstrated in the studio. These you can put into the video. My producer, Doug, and I filmed this particular video on a special set where we had access to a real section of a plane. We were able to film the bag close up, show someone putting it into the overhead compartment, and display how the wheels turn so you can easily maneuver down a narrow airplane aisle. We also went to a hotel so we could film someone rolling the bag past someone else in a narrow hallway. These kind of live-action lifestyle shots are invaluable.

Usually people hire someone to film the videos for them, but as you probably guessed, I like to be part of the process. I create a video for almost every item I sell. I think it's important. I've been working with Doug for fifteen years. We try to shoot two to three products in a day to make the most of the house or other location we rent and the models and videographer we hire. It's important to make the most use of your money. While the shoot is laborious, I find editing to be really fun. I feel like it helps me tell the story about my product. Doug can do the editing right on his PC, so he comes to my office and we sit and do it together. We watch the raw footage, I pick my favorite shots, and we put it together to tell a story.

So, six months of planning and preparation are behind me as I walk into the QVC studios at 4 p.m. ready to prep for my 8 p.m. show. We tend to talk and laugh a lot, so the floor managers sometimes have to shush us and tell us to use our inside voices. They tell us we're having too much fun. This is pretty much how we are together all the time. I have a great team. QVC supplies tables and gurneys for different sets. There is a huge warehouse at the studio called "Product Central" where QVC has stocked two of each item being shown that day, but I bring my own propped products.

A day or two before the show, the coordinating producer and I will go through the whole hour show on the phone and review to make sure everyone knows everyone's needs, such as which sets we'll use for which items. There are two bedroom sets, three kitchen sets, a living room set, a spa set, a fashion and jewelry set, a multipurpose room, and so on. All this type of information gets put into a product blueprint, a document that accompanies every single product that airs on QVC explaining every detail anyone might need to know about that product, from what props and tables are necessary, to what set will be used, to what type of camera is needed. It goes to the person in charge of the product's brand in broadcasting. All of that information stays in the blueprint forever, so that anyone who reads it knows exactly what to do for that product.

One surprising fact is that when you're selling on air, there aren't very many people on set with you. The cameras are robotic and operated from a control room up above; only essential personnel are on the floor. There are production assistants—people who help move gurneys, cameras, and monitors around—but they're working, not focusing on you per se. It's a 24-hour live show. They've seen all this before. That's why, even in the beginning, I never felt uncomfortable. It's not like in the movies, when an actor will look out from a film set and you'll see through his eyes a director, four cameramen, and a bunch of assistants and other people staring back. It doesn't feel like anyone is watching, even though in reality millions are. I forget about it until the customers themselves start calling to talk to me, which is so much fun.

There are usually a few minutes to kill once we're set up before we go on air. I'm pretty social and generally use this time to chat with everyone at the studio. My team jokingly complains that they are constantly losing me at the last second, right when I'm supposed to get miced, and Dan finally put a GPS on my phone so he could track me down. It's a big studio. Yet I always know my show times, and in seventeen years I've never been late for a show. As soon as I get the signal, all of my attention is on the cameras 100 percent as I move from set to set selling various products. All along I can tell how products are doing because I can often see the sales numbers coming in real time on a monitor in front of me.

There is no changing the sell if the numbers aren't what you want them to be. Hard selling isn't allowed on QVC, and your customer wouldn't appreciate it, anyway. You just have to hope that all the work you did beforehand translates the way you wanted it to on air. No one is perfect. Sometimes you get on air and realize you should have shown something else, or that you could improve your demo. If you make your numbers to get reordered you can evolve, enhance, and improve for the next time. It's an ongoing process.

Since I'm in from out of town, QVC makes the most use of my time by scheduling several shows within a 24-hour period.

Also, if I'm selling a product at a special price for that day only, they can maximize that opportunity by scheduling several shows in one day. Often my show will air on Friday night at 8 p.m. Eastern Standard Time, an hour before *Shark Tank* airs on the East Coast. Once I'm done with the 8 p.m. show, I don't go home. I dash to the green room, where I start live tweeting during *Shark Tank* from 9 to 10 p.m. During that time, my team and I will relax and let loose! Sometimes we'll bring in pizzas or chicken cheese steaks from three different places and have a throwdown, each of us judging whose food is best. I order crazy amounts of food, not because we're starving but because it's fun. I like to live life *abbondanza*!

Sometimes we'll have another show at 1 a.m., which airs just after the West Coast airing of *Shark Tank*. By the time we get home, it's about 3:30 a.m. It's now been a 20-hour day and we're all ready to crash. It can be a long, long, day, but it's also incredibly gratifying.

OTHER SELLING VENUES

Infomercials

Like the home shopping channels, infomercials are great venues to showcase demonstrable products and sell directly to consumers. Some of them become cultural touchstones, launching iconic taglines along with their products, like the Ginsu Knife's "But wait, there's more!" or Ron Popeil's "Set it and forget it!" For the right product and the right pitchman, like Billy Mays and George Foreman, infomercials can be direct roads to fame and fortune. But as we explored in Chapter 5, they can also be fraught with risk.

Legitimate infomercial companies can help you make inroads into the market and pave the way to getting an order with a retailer or a spot on one of the home shopping networks. But too many have taken advantage of new entrepreneurs' desperation to get on the air, seducing them with the promise of millions of eyes. Many are legitimate, but I've also heard stories and seen circumstances where they are not. If a company tells you they love your product and they will make an infomercial for you and know how to test the airtime, and all you have to do is put up $25,000 to $100,000, look out. Some inventors are willing to take the risk, thinking that they'll make more money that way than if they put more of the risk on the infomercial company. Often, however, they lose their money. It's smarter to let the infomercial company, which is expert at this, handle the production and pay the costs.

I was once introduced to a terrific, creative inventor who had managed to get himself in the hole to the tune of about $600,000. I thought his product was great and that he was smart, clever, and genuine. I thought maybe I could help him get out of the hole and we could both make some money in the process. I launched his item on QVC and it sold great. He started making money and was able to cover his debts. But then a friend approached him and suggested that he could make even more money if they worked together to produce an infomercial. He didn't go in blindly. He did his homework; he spoke to me and listened to my advice. But in the end, he decided that he stood a good chance of succeeding and went ahead with the infomercial.

It didn't work. He didn't lose a ton of money because his friend produced the piece, but he was still on the hook for the air time, and that wasn't cheap. Anxious to make his money back (and probably just as anxious to prove that the dream was still alive), he jumped when a company contacted him about professionally producing an infomercial. He figured that his big mistake had been doing it himself; surely he would succeed now that he was working with pros. That infomercial didn't work, either, and he descended deeper into debt. Too often, entrepreneurs get so obsessed with chasing the dream that they realize they've been chasing it in circles only when it's too late.

Hiring a celebrity endorser is another trap a lot of entrepreneurs fall into. It does not help you to pay a lot of money for a celebrity to endorse your product unless he or she is somehow a natural fit for the product. Hiring a male Olympic athlete to sell your jewelry won't sell a single gemstone. The relationship of product to pitchman has to make sense to the public.

There's a right way to do an infomercial and a wrong way. If you're going to take the risk, partner up with a company that will produce it for you, even though that means you may make a smaller percentage on your sales. If you've produced a quality infomercial with trustworthy partners, and the item still doesn't sell, then you know it's probably not an infomercial product.

Mail-Order Catalogs

Even in the Internet age, catalogs are a billion-dollar business, and there's no reason you shouldn't be a part of it. Just as people love to watch television salespeople demonstrate products on TV, a lot of people still enjoy flipping through glossy pages full of beautifully photographed products and being able to order at their leisure. Many people save catalogs and go back to them later. You reach out to a catalog buyer the same way as you would to any other buyer. One resource might be *The Catalog of Catalogs*, fourth edition. It's like the mail-order catalog version of *The Chain Store Guide*.

E-commerce

Selling on your own website will always earn you the greatest amount of net profit per sale. In fact, Web sales can make up to

30 percent or more of people's business. You can hire a designer to create a website for you, but there are other resources, like DesignCrowd or Fiverr, which can put you in touch with freelancers at reasonable rates and where you can also find people to help you. Once your website is up, it'll be a heck of a lot of work to keep it up, so be prepared or be sure to have staff on hand to help.

In addition, just putting up a website isn't enough to direct traffic to go there. There are many companies that can help you with search engine optimization (SEO). Doing cross-promotions; Google Ads; utilizing social media through Facebook, Twitter, Pinterest, and Instagram—whatever you can do to raise awareness of your product and your website, you should actively do all the time. Make sure you have a great website that clearly explains your product, and if you can, try to sell direct through it.

Do what you can to encourage people to post great ratings and reviews on your website. Testimonials are extremely powerful and effective marketing tools.

Amazon is the mother of all e-commerce sites, and Etsy is well known as the online source for all things indie, artsy, and crafty; but over the past few years, services called e-commerce website builders, also known as shopping cart designers, are gaining on them. Currently, the most talked-about ones seem to be BigCommerce, Volusion, Big-Cartel, 3dcart, Shopify, and Magento. All pretty much promise to accomplish the same thing: to allow businesses to build their own online storefront without having to go to all the trouble of designing and building a website through an expensive Web designer. Each varies in scope and has its own particular benefits.

For example, BigCommerce is known for excellent SEO configuration and ease of use, whereas BigCartel is specifically designed to handle small businesses selling fewer than one hundred products.

Take advantage of any online initiatives you can find. YouTube can be a terrific sales tool if you can figure out creative ways to get people to go to your YouTube channel. Pinterest is a fantastic place to showcase certain items, since it attracts a huge number of shoppers, so make your presence known there if you can. Do whatever you can to get your product out in front of consumers. Think of the Internet as the online equivalent of driving around town with a giant sign flashing on top of your car. And while you're out there selling, make sure you keep talking, too. Just as a great demo can inspire consumers to buy, engaging with customers and building buzz around your product is a great way to make sure the word gets out.

BEYOND BRICK-AND-MORTAR TO-DO LIST:

❑ Determine your product is demonstrable and therefore a good candidate for TV sales.

❑ If you have a highly demonstrable product, tailor your pitch to accommodate television buyers' concerns.

❑ Hire someone to build your website or shopping cart site, or start building it on your own.

❑ Film a video of your product to post on your website and any other online selling or marketing locations.

11

MARKETING THAT REALLY WORKS

"What counts is not necessarily the size of the dog in the fight,
but the size of the fight in the dog."

—AUTHOR UNKNOWN

BECAUSE I'M ON TELEVISION ALL THE TIME AND HAVE BEEN FROM the very beginning, I have not found it necessary to pay for marketing. Television shopping channels are the ideal medium because they give you a selling, advertising, and marketing platform all rolled into one. Selling on television keeps your product in front of your customers' eyes far longer than when they're browsing through a store or even watching an ordinary 30-second commercial. In addition, television demos reinforce your consumers' in-store experience because, after so much exposure, there's little chance consumers can pass your product on a retail shelf and not *recognize* it.

In the past, when the only marketing choices available to entrepreneurs were TV, radio, and print, and people's main daily source of news and entertainment was the television, there was little need for me to invest in marketing because I already had a presence where it mattered most. The advent of social media, however, flung open a door that had previously been unavailable. Now with the onset of this alternative and immediate source of exposure, I could talk to my existing and potential customers even when I wasn't on the air. That created a definite marketing opportunity worth pursuing. More important, I was thrilled to have an open line straight to my QVC customers, and I genuinely welcomed the chance to talk freely with them. I am where I am because of them. I love hearing their testimonials on air, and in more recent years, engaging with them on my website, Facebook, and Twitter. And now I get to do it with *Shark Tank* viewers, too!

HOW TO BE SOCIAL

There has simply never been a better way than social media to inexpensively get your message out to large masses of people. Perhaps even more important, social media provide you with a great way to directly connect with your audience and make them feel personally involved with you and your brand.

You don't want to use social media exclusively to push and sell. That's boring, and most people will start to ignore you. You need to mix things up—a little selling here, a little fun storytelling there, a picture one day, a video the next. Make sure to infuse all of your sites with variety, humor, and authenticity. I try to post about twice a day. In my experience, this technique seems to strike the ideal balance between staying on people's radar and not saturating their feeds or causing overexposure. On Twitter, you may consider tweeting a little more frequently, since it's easy to miss posts in the torrent of content that flows every minute.

I use social media to get the word out about my appearances

in the media, my new products, and my upcoming QVC shows or newest *Shark Tank* season. On Fridays I typically post videos about my thoughts on that night's new *Shark Tank* episode. I also find it effective to run contests and giveaways to pump up excitement about some of my favorite products. It's a way of giving back to my loyal followers and customers. People love when I post photos of what goes on behind the scenes at QVC and *Shark Tank*.

I also like to post photos of me doing totally ordinary things, like playing golf, traveling to new places, or cooking in my kitchen. A great post was during the summer of 2013, when Dan and I were visiting a friend's house for the 4th of July. My niece looked down and said, "What's that?" We saw three little pink things on the ground. They were moving. I posted a photo of them because I didn't know what they were, and we got thousands of answers within minutes. They were baby squirrels, hours old, which had fallen out of a tree. My Facebook followers knew just what to do, and I'm happy to say the squirrels are doing fine.

These kind of posts let my fans get to know me better and build a sense of community. I also post many quotes and words of wisdom, not just because I find them meaningful but also because people tell me that these quotes inspire them and help fuel their desire to keep following their dreams, or pick them up after a hard day. The world can be a rough place, and as we've discussed throughout this book, the entrepreneurial road can be challenging and hard to maneuver. I love knowing that I can be a source of positive energy and encouragement in the midst of all the noise and busyness and stress. Social media give me a way to connect with my audience, give them a reason to trust me and get to know me, and reveal that when I step away from the cameras, I'm no different from anyone else.

Social media are all about what's happening right now. Think of your website as your highlights reel, where fans can come to see your greatest hits and spend some time investigating what you've done in the past, what you're doing currently, and what's coming up. Think of your social media sites as places to share things in the moment. Your website is one-size-fits-all and your home base, your social media can be broad, or you can use ads to target certain demographics, ages, and interests. In this way, you can make sure that your brand is always relevant to your customers, and can find ways to remind them of the role you can play in their lives.

In addition, there's no better gauge than social media to tell you which marketing messages are working and which ones are not. If you get applause in the form of shares, retweets, and pins, and engagement in the form of comments and replies, you know you've struck a chord. If you post a piece of content and hear crickets, you know you've missed your mark.

WHICH SOCIAL SITE IS RIGHT FOR YOU?

There are many social media sites to choose from, but the ones I prefer most are also the most popular.

Facebook

Surely you set up a Facebook business page as soon as you decided you were going to follow through with your dream and bring your new invention to market. If you didn't, though, go do it right now. Your customers are there, waiting for you. As of the end of 2012, nearly two-thirds of the adults online used Facebook. It gives businesses an unparalleled way to establish a relationship with their customers and keep them apprised of where the brand is growing and how they can be a part of it. As with all social media, the most effective way to use Facebook is to put out posts that not only engage your fans and let them know you're thinking of them but also makes them want to share your posts with others.

To get the most out of Facebook, you want to focus less on quantity and more on quality, because the key to a great Facebook presence is high engagement. You need to post things that inspire people to like, comment, and share what you post, not just read it. That's why I say things like, "LIKE this post if you're ready for Season Five of *Shark Tank!*" As another example, Marc Newburger and Jeffrey Simon, creators of the Drop Stop, created a shareable icon that people could post on each other's walls. It allowed the user to fill in the appropriate names to personalize it, so that, for example, Sarah could post on John's wall: "Sarah just filled John's crack with Drop Stop." People who received the icons thought they were funny, and they were then generally intrigued enough to click on the icon, which took them to the Drop Stop website.

Twitter

Unlike Facebook, you don't have to know or even be "friends" with someone on Twitter to interact with them, which automatically changes the dynamic between you and your audience. It has a younger audience than Facebook, and its hashtag culture demands that businesses stay extremely up to date on trends so they can appropriately label their tweets to get the biggest reach. I use Twitter to disseminate some of the same content that I post on Facebook, but I also like to use it to give people insight into my thoughts. I love live tweeting during episodes of *Shark Tank*. I do it every Friday night (@LoriGreiner). It's a great way for me to turn the recorded episode into a live event and communicate directly with our *Shark Tank* followers while the show is playing. Often the viewers' comments are so funny we laugh out loud.

What's nice about Twitter is that you don't have to wait for people to come to you to talk about your product; you can go straight to them. Searching Twitter via Twitter trends, or clicking on hashtags to see who else is talking about a certain topic relevant to your brand or product, is a great way to find new customers and engage them in conversation. The idea is not to engage them so you can sell to them; it's to engage them so that they decide you have something interesting to say and you're worth following. The sale will, it is hoped, happen later, when you tweet something so catchy, profound, or so intriguing that your follower finally heads over to your site to see if, maybe, today is the day to try out your product.

Twitter, Facebook, and all social media are addictive and satisfying for their immediate gratification and instant feedback, but as a successful business tool, they are platforms that require time and patience. Maybe you'll immediately see sales when you tweet that your product is now available in six new colors, or maybe you won't. Most important is that people like you and your voice along with your product, so that they're interested in staying engaged with you.

Pinterest

Pinterest is synonymous with eye candy. It's a site primarily, though not exclusively, populated by women. Pinterest is where these women go to collect the images of things they love, things they admire, and things they want to buy, particularly food, fashion, and home décor, although other kinds of products can do well there, too.

Pinterest isn't as good a venue for social engagement as is Facebook or Twitter; it has comment capabilities, but that's not as popular here. Repins and likes serve as great barometers of how well your product resonates with the Pinterest viewers. If you don't see much action, it might be because your photograph isn't good enough (Pinterest photos often look like they were taken by professionals), your description isn't appealing enough, or maybe there are too many other things in that category.

By getting people to repin your pin, you will get people to be aware of it and that can lead to great sales. It's like a lush, streamlined catalog. But unlike any catalog, you don't have to pick up the phone or head to your computer in order to place an order. You're already there. And most of those beautiful Pinterest photographs link straight to a vendor's website where you can immediately make a purchase. It's a supremely easy and efficient way for businesses to show off their wares and gain the attention of new potential customers.

Another interesting way to use Pinterest is to create boards that can reflect the various sides of your personality or your brand. Of course, I have a board dedicated exclusively to my products, but as I do on Facebook, I love to share inspirational quotes and things I think are beautiful or interesting, so I also have a board where I post nothing but those. It gives me another way in which to engage with people. Consumers who are interested in what I do on *Shark Tank* or are interested in my products will also check out my Pinterest page to see what I have going on there.

Rick Hopper of ReadeRest has a board where he posts images of products that he finds clever, useful, or funny. The board doesn't do anything to specifically market his own product, but it is a lot of fun to scroll through, and anything that can keep people connected to your Pinterest page for more than a millisecond has value. Remember, as immediately gratifying as social media can be, when it comes to marketing on these platforms and converting brand awareness to sales, slow and steady wins the race.

Reddit

Another site where some entrepreneurs I've worked with have gotten good traction is Reddit, specifically a Q&A forum called AMA (Ask Me Anything). Reddit is a social media site where communities center around topics rather than individual brands. Because of this distinction, it's not the best place for self-promotion, because the site limits the number of links you can submit from any one source. Individuals submit links, and community members vote the links up or down. The popularity of links determines their placements on the site, with the most popular links making it to the front page, where they receive the most visibility.

An AMA is essentially an opportunity to schedule an interview with members of your community. Of course, your fans have access to you through Facebook, Pinterest, and Twitter, but with this format you're basically giving your audience a chunk of your undivided time, which in this busy day and age is quite a novelty. When I've done Reddits, I've found that people love asking me questions and hearing my answers, and I love hearing what they have to say, too. Again, this is not the place to sell. But if you launch an intelligent conversation and become an integral part of communities that revolve around topics related to your brand, you can gain a lot of awareness.

Google+ Hangouts

Hangouts are a lot like video versions of Reddit AMA's. Users can gather for group chats and videoconferences, which can then sync to other sites for broader dissemination. For example, when I did a hangout, I synced it with my Twitter and Facebook accounts so that anyone there could watch the hangout live even if they weren't on Google+. In addition, those Twitter and Facebook viewers could send in their own questions, which I then answered live.

WHY I LOVE SOCIAL MEDIA

The thing I love best about the social media isn't so much what they allow me to give in the form of information, but what they allow me to receive. Hearing from my customers affirms my faith in humanity. I'm amazed by the diversity of the people who follow me on social media. They are all different ages, genders, and backgrounds—it's fun getting to know them and hearing about their lives. Talking to them proves to me that overall people are really good and caring. From a business perspective, it's great to hear my customers' opinions and concerns in real time. For example, when I'm creating new products, I can ask fans about what color choices they'd prefer or what design details would be most useful. I can ask people how they felt about a deal I did or didn't make on the last *Shark Tank* episode. Their comments and responses to my questions are always entertaining, inspiring, and downright hilarious. Plus, they help me stay aware of what is important to people and what is most on their minds.

While the social media serve my business well by allowing me to market to my audience, they also serve me personally by helping me feel more connected to my fans and reassuring me that I'm giving them what they want and need. That's the secret to successful social media marketing. Yes, it's a great marketing tool, but it only works if your primary aim is to build community and engage with people. *Engaging* does not mean posting or tweeting links to your webpage or e-commerce site every six minutes. Engaging means really being interested in hearing what your consumers have to say. It means joining communities and contributing to them. It means sharing other people's content when you think your audience would enjoy it as much as you did, even if that means sharing the spotlight. It means liking or favoriting when they tweet or post something you like. It's a lot more about give and take, and asking and listening, than it is about pushing and promoting.

One person who has gotten a lot of press for his personal, seamless social media marketing is Justin Timberlake. In particular, he seems to have mastered the art of making his fans feel like he's speaking directly in his own voice, not hiding behind a PR firm. If you spend enough time on his Facebook page, and especially his Twitter feed, where he intersperses album promos with birthday greetings to his friends, asides to fellow performers, and direct responses to fans, you come away feeling that you know him.

While there are plenty of direct sales pitches, there are far more questions, teasers, photographs, and behind-the-scenes revelations. To help promote his first studio release in seven years, he hosted a scavenger hunt, hiding signed copies of a vinyl version of his new album in locations across the country. Clues to the locations were posted as Instagram photos. People who raced to the locations and found the albums had to show record label reps the hashtag that accompanied the Twitter clue to prove they weren't just lucky passersby. By all accounts, his strategic use of social media was one of the most successful album marketing campaigns in recent history, resulting in first-week sales of almost a million copies, a rare number in today's fractured music industry.

Yet there are lots of talented pop stars out there who tweet and post and "engage," but who don't see those kinds of sales upon their album's release. Of course, none of Timberlake's efforts would amount to anything if he weren't also producing a

> You can't just launch a promotion like a contest, sweepstakes, or giveaway on your social media sites—there is a whole body of law in this area, so the sites generally have extremely strict rules about what you can do and how it needs to be set up. You need to be aware of these regulations. I strongly advise you to discuss your plans with an attorney who specializes in social media before attempting to run any kind of game, sweepstakes, promotion, or contest on a social media site. It would be terrible for you to have to take your page or account down because you did something wrong.

superb product. But what really made the difference, according to executives in music and marketing industries, was his tireless and genuine efforts to connect with his fans.

You may not be Justin Timberlake, but there is no reason why inventors and entrepreneurs with fabulous products to sell can't model some of their marketing efforts after his to gain a loyal following and enhanced brand awareness.

OTHER MARKETING OPTIONS

ONLINE FORUMS Long before Reddit, there were online forums, and many still exist and are going strong. They tend to appeal to niche audiences. Gaming is a highly popular topic for online forums, but they exist for all kinds of interests, from parenting to vegetarianism. The Drop Stop "Boyz" discovered that there are online forums for every make of car, with enormous followings. Once they started interacting with the community—sharing ideas, trading stories, offering advice, but never selling—eventually members started finding out about their product and asked for more information. All that community building generally puts people in a positive, supportive frame of mind, and once one member tried the Drop Stop and endorsed it, the rest flocked to try it themselves.

BUYSELLADS.COM BuySellAds.com allows you to pay very little for various social media–related boosts, like getting ad placement on an influential blog or paying people with large Twitter followings to tweet for you.

CELEBRITIES It's a long shot, but getting your product into the right celebrity hands can sometimes do amazing things for your brand. One magazine photograph of a celebrity using your product, and your website may see a tremendous boost in traffic. Remember, the rule for matching celebrity to product holds true here as it does in infomercials: it has to make sense. A better strategy than spending a lot of time and money courting celebrities is to make sure that your individual customers love it, and encourage them to share their positive experiences with others, both in person and through social media.

Celebrities find out about many products the same way everyone else does—they see them on TV, they bump into a friend who uses them, they read their cousin's status update about them. That's when they decide they want those products for themselves. Kelly Preston told me that her husband John Travolta was watching QVC one day when we were both on. I came on to sell my weekender bag, and next thing she knew, he wanted three. I was psyched. I like John Travolta, and he's a pilot! As far as I know, no one has photographed him using the bags, but you have to think he spends a lot of time around other people who travel frequently. All it would take is one compliment on the bag to start a conversation around it, which might then lead to another sale.

Do the heavy lifting first—make a quality product—and as word of mouth builds, you'll have a better chance of getting it into celebrity hands. For the record, on the occasion when you can get a celebrity endorsement, it can have a big impact. One day my company got a call from an editor at *O* magazine telling us that they wanted to see my Silver Safekeeper in the letter "o." A couple of weeks later, they requested thirty more boxes in a variety of letters. They were going to be given away as party favors for a client in California.

Later we found out that the party was at Oprah's house! It turned out that Gayle King had seen the Silver Safekeeper and showed it to Oprah, and they had decided it would be a perfect party favor. We were flattered, honored, and grateful, and even more so when they featured it as one of Oprah's "Favorite Things" in the magazine. Getting a thumbs-up from Oprah resulted in the single largest boost in sales of this product.

SOCIAL MARKETING COMPLEMENTS TRADITIONAL MARKETING

With so much of this chapter devoted to emphasizing the benefits of social media, you might think that no one need ever invest in traditional marketing avenues like television, print, or radio anymore. Not at all. Traditional marketing works, and works really well. However, if your funds are limited, it doesn't make sense to spend a fortune when you can reach your consumers for free, or at least for significantly less than you'd pay for a print ad or infomercial.

Social media marketing will cost you far less than any traditional marketing platforms possibly could, and you could potentially reach more people. If you do opt to pay for some traditional marketing, and you want to make the most of your investment, it is imperative that you figure out ways to integrate social media into it. Now that the vast majority of people turn to the Internet and their electronic devices for their news and entertainment, social media marketing must be a main focus of your marketing strategy.

You have to make sure that your marketing reaches your consumers whether they're online or off. Ideally, your online marketing will often highlight events surrounding your brand and other ways in which consumers can interact with your product out in the real world, and your traditional marketing will reinforce your online presence and remind consumers to look for you when they are there, too. For example, if you print postcards to hand out at trade shows, street festivals, or sales events, make sure that your website is clearly listed, and that you include icons indicating your presence on Facebook, Twitter, Pinterest, and any other social media platforms you use. Many businesses use testimonials taken from their social media sites when writing ads or marketing copy.

MARKETING OPENS DOORS

The Internet is your friend. If you're having trouble breaking down doors and getting into retail venues, concentrate on boosting your online networks and fans, so that buyers will take you seriously. Build a fantastic website. Create a Facebook page, and start posting lots of interesting, colorful updates. Tweet to build followers and create a community around your product or brand. Try initiating a Groupon offer, if appropriate. Sell on Etsy. Do whatever it takes to build traction and hype. Can you get your product into the right celebrity's hands? Can you get a local television personality to interview you or feature your product on a show? Use all the resources and all the creativity you have to get your product in the public eye.

Get the word-of-mouth machine cranking, so that your product is talked about and seen as widely as possible. Create a perfect storm. Hit every marketing platform as hard and fast as possible. I've blitzed the market with almost every product I've introduced. This strategy has worked for me, and I've seen it work for many others, too. No matter what your product, if you can corner the market before someone else, even if the competition eventually tries to knock you off, it's your product's name that will be on everyone's minds. And once you've got brand recognition and loyalty, you'll have almost everything you need for success, because buyers don't like to turn their backs on products that are already selling well.

MARKETING TO-DO LIST:

- ☐ Set up a Facebook page.

- ☐ Set up a Twitter account.

- ☐ Set up a Pinterest page, if applicable.

- ☐ Research and follow some of your favorite brands to see what they're doing online and how it's effective.

- ☐ Create a shareable branded piece of content like an icon, logo, or image with a catchy phrase that will entertain or inspire people enough to compel them to pass it on to others.

12

KEEP THE DREAM GOING—EXPAND AND DIVERSIFY

YOU DID IT. YOUR PRODUCT IS SELLING IN STORES AND ONLINE. Your factory is going full speed ahead. Your marketing efforts are helping you reach more and more fans and customers every day. You have achieved the dream. You're done!

Actually, if you're like most entrepreneurs, you're not done. This really is only just the beginning. As I said in the start of this book, if you can create one amazing product and build a sustainable business with it, you have reason to be proud. Not many people get to see their invention make its way into the mass market and experience the elation of creating something that makes people's lives just a little bit better, whether it's by providing the solution to a problem, improving or enhancing their space with a new design, or even just giving them a reason to laugh.

For most inventors, however, the satisfying taste of success will only whet the appetite (as well as that of your buyers) for more. If you managed to bring a product to market successfully once, why couldn't you do it again? You can, and it'll be easier the second time. And the best thing about it is that you don't even have to start from scratch.

I hadn't even thought about creating another product after just six months of selling my jewelry organizer. It started selling well as soon as it appeared on the shelves at JCPenney and other brick-and-mortar retailers. It was after it appeared on the Home Shopping Network, however, and they could barely keep it in stock, that my Home Shopping Network buyer sat me down to ask me what more I had planned—what other new products were coming? More?

There was nothing more. I hadn't ever thought about creating another product. I hadn't planned to branch out with other inventions—I just wanted to make the best earring organizer possible and be successful with it. Her question took me completely off guard. But as we discussed earlier, buyers have a business to run, too, and they're always looking for new and exciting products. I started to get excited. Yes! Of course I could think of more products! My mind started going and it hasn't stopped.

Once I got over my initial surprise, the next product almost invented itself. I simply added an interchangeable bracelet bar and necklace bar to the original organizer. It sold great, too. We started getting customer requests for a cover for it. Done. Within a few more months, I created my first spinning cosmetic organizer, which went on HSN, and into Linens 'n Things under their private label.

USE YOUR ORIGINAL PRODUCT FOR INSPIRATION

There is no need to panic if until now you have invested all of your energy into developing one perfect product and have given little thought to anything else. Add-ons and extensions can be an inventor's personal gold mine, especially if you have patented your product and technology. You don't need to look far for new product ideas. Stick to what you know and create more market-able, successful products along the same lines of what is already working. Start with add-ons and companion pieces to enhance your idea that is already selling well.

Many successful entrepreneurs and companies have followed this business model. After Aaron Krause hit it big with his Scrub Daddy cleaning sponges, we started thinking about what other products we could make out of this special patented foam that no one else could make or use but us. The result was an extension product called the Scrub Daisy, a wand filled with soap, with a little foam flower at the end that fit perfectly into most glasses so that the bottom could be properly cleaned. Soon we were coming out with scented Scrub Daddies and ones in different colors. And who knows, maybe we'll adapt Aaron's invention to clean items well beyond what can fit into a kitchen sink, like floors, cars, or windows. After all, he was washing a car when the idea for the Scrub Daddy hit him!

Once you create a product that succeeds, the possibilities are endless. As time goes on, you can learn more about your market and consumer demand, you can enhance your technology, and you can use that knowledge to make improvements and to fuel an endless stream of creation and innovation. I started with one earring organizer, and today I have launched over 400 products. I started with one in each arena, and expanded from small to large, from a full cheval-style mirror with jewelry storage inside that holds 350 pieces, to a double-sided spinning mirror cabinet that holds more than 750 pieces. When you become good at one thing, it's easy to make more and more in the same genre.

Expand upon a Great Idea

There's no reason to reinvent the wheel every time you want to branch out beyond your initial product or into new markets. Your invention provides a service to one market, so think about how you can adapt that same service to another one. For example, once I had a full line of various jewelry organizers, I looked around and saw that the cosmetics market didn't have any good organizational solutions, either. I remembered my mother's sink strewn about with all the compacts, brushes, eye shadows, and lipsticks. I had created a patented deluxe Silver Safekeeper jewelry box with swing-out doors that allows you to see up to 350 pieces of jewelry in an instant. Nothing piles on top of each other; it's all beautifully displayed like a fine store display, but at home.

It was so popular that I decided to adapt the exact same type of design with the swing-out doors for cosmetics. So I created my deluxe cosmetic organizer, and it too is a great-selling item in my line. Every time I have a concept that works, I think about what else I can do with it. Throughout my entire career, products have just snowballed. With the massive success of the Fill-A-Bowl at QVC, Michael's craft store, and many other places, I created a Fill-a-Jar, a Fill-a-Tray, a Fill-a-Trivet, a Fill-a-Frame, and a Fill-a-Fork and Spoon. The Fill-A items became a huge line of their own. It was the same thing with my closet organizers, my travel bags, and so on. I never tried to invent a need; I simply listened to what people complained about the most, and then invented a solution.

Do What You Know

I specifically targeted my products to women because it was a market that I knew, and because a large percent of the viewers of QVC were women. I was also constantly hearing from women about how grateful they were to finally have products that helped them eradicate the clutter and disorder that kept making its way into their busy lives. And what are the five purchases most women make above all else? Clothes, shoes, makeup, jewelry, and food. So it made sense to focus on creating products that were related to those five categories.

BIDE YOUR TIME BEFORE BRANCHING OUT TOO FAR

I stuck to making plastic products for a long time because I knew how injection molding worked. It took several years before I decided the business and my brand were entrenched enough to risk experimenting with new materials and markets. It's extremely important not to get so caught up in the high of success that you throw caution to the wind and overextend yourself. If you started selling an unbelievable pair of scissors that became the next hot gadget, you might consider branching out into gardening shears or kitchen knives. Paper shredders, however, might be a risky stretch unless you've got a ready-made "in." In the beginning of your career, don't be afraid to branch out, but stick with familiar mediums and markets. As you grow and succeed, you will make the connections you need to successfully step into new arenas.

Eventually, I did start creating products out of wood overseas. They weren't too risky, for at their core they were still extensions of my previously successful lines. People really appreciated my Deluxe Silver Safekeeper antitarnish jewelry box and I knew they loved the earring organizer. Why not take both and turn it into one? So I made a box, and enhanced its aesthetic appeal by making it out of wood. It had sliding earring stands, and the entire box would swivel open all at once so you could see your whole collection at once.

When it did well, I started thinking about how to make it

even better. So far I had created products that sat on women's bathroom counters or vanities. But what could we do that was bigger and better? My customers were big jewelry lovers and wanted *even more* storage. That's when I designed my full-length mirror Gold and Silver Safekeeper Jewelry Cabinet. It's still wood, and it still incorporates everything people loved about the earring organizer. And like the jewelry box, everything is in clear view and hanging like a store display, except now it is a cheval-style, full-length floor-standing mirror that opens up to reveal a jewelry cabinet inside.

The next step was to create the same cabinet that would hang on the wall. On both, the mirrored door locks and hides your entire jewelry collection, up to 350 pieces. It has earring bars, hooks for necklaces, shelves for bracelets, and slots for rings. It looks completely different from my original tabletop product, but in reality it's a first cousin. But customers wanted even *more*! So I made the big daddy of them all, a full-length jewelry cabinet with the same cheval-style standing mirror, but this one spins on a base and has doors on each side. One side holds all your neck-laces, the other side holds all your earrings, rings, cuffs, pins, and more. It holds more than 800 pieces, all in clear view.

It's like a formula: (1) start with one concept, design an ex-tension or add-on to create a second one; (2) now blend the two to make a third. In this way, you can ultimately grow your busi-ness by developing extensions of products that have already seen success and have established a track record.

CONCLUSION

*"The world always seems brighter when you've just
made something that wasn't there before."*

—NEIL GAIMAN

THE DAYS MAY BE LONG AND THE WORK MAY BE HARD, BUT I'M
happy. I love doing what I do. There are so many benefits. When
I accepted the opportunity to appear on *Shark Tank*, I saw it as a
mere extension of the kind of mentoring, partnering, and investing I have done throughout my career. I had been on television
for years; I thought it would just be a little more of the same. And
yet it has changed my life.

I didn't set out to become a public personality, but I take
my new role seriously. I want to be a good role model. When
parents tell me that they let their kids watch *Shark Tank* because
they think their children can learn something valuable from it,
or that their kids have been inspired to become entrepreneurs
after watching the show, that's particularly touching. It's nice

that people say *Shark Tank* is a show they can watch together as a family.

Becoming an entrepreneur seems to be a growing trend. Universities offer classes in entrepreneurship now, and I've heard that high schools are starting to offer entrepreneurship in their curriculum as well. It's exciting to think about all the innovative, creative ideas currently percolating that will one day explode onto the market and maybe change the way we all live. People come up to me and tell me how times have been tough, that job security doesn't exist, but that entrepreneurship has given them the power to take control of their lives and destiny. That's incredibly good news.

I believe we are all on earth for a purpose. Being kind, giving back, contributing—these are important values I try to uphold. We're supposed to do good, and if this is one of the ways I can do my part, I'm happy for the opportunity.

That's what being an entrepreneur is all about—grabbing opportunity. The most exciting thing about that is that when you step through a door of opportunity, other doors start to open. If there is anything you take away from this book, it is this: You can make anything happen if you put your mind to it. Everything you've learned from these pages will help you as you take steps toward getting your invention onto retail shelves, QVC, or even *Shark Tank*. There's no such thing as a yellow brick road. You're going to stumble into potholes and maybe even into manholes, but when you get yourself out, you'll be a smarter, stronger, wiser entrepreneur.

You can achieve your dream of turning your brilliant idea into a reality if you're willing to do whatever it takes, literally. Inform yourself about your product and your market so that you're a walking encyclopedia of facts and figures. When things don't go the way you thought they would, find another path to reach the same end. Do not take no for an answer. If your idea is as good as you think it is, there is always a way to make your dreams happen. Reach for the stars; you might just catch one.

Bringing an invention to life isn't the only entrepreneurial path to bliss, or the only path to happiness and success. It just happens to be a wonderful and rewarding one for those with the stamina, determination, and courage to pursue it. That is you, isn't it?

ACKNOWLEDGMENTS

There are so many people to thank for helping to make this book happen and for supporting me along my journey. First and foremost I want to thank Stephanie Land, my writing partner, who helped me to put together this book. She's brillant, a great person, and was ever so patient with my incessant changes. I thank you!

I want to thank Ryan Doherty and his team at Ballantine for their belief in me and all their care and efforts on behalf of this book. I also want to thank Joel Gotler, my literary agent, for all of his help.

Of course, I want to thank my husband, Dan (see dedication).

I thank my parents, grandparents, in-laws, aunts, and family for their love, believing in me, and for the values they instilled in me.

I want to thank everyone involved and a part of my incredible team! And a special thanks to Coopie, Ann, Dale, Mannie, Heidi, Patrice, Jack, Phyllis, Cathy, and Julia whose support and devotion have meant so much!

A huge special thank-you to Brien, for your years of friendship. It means more than you can ever know!

I want to thank QVC for their partnership and my many

years there. It's been a fantastic journey! Bern, for your first piece of advice sixteen years ago!

I also want to thank Mark Burnett and the producers of *Shark Tank* (Clay, Holly, Mark, Lisa, John, and your teams), ABC, and Sony, for having me be a part of this fantastic experience and for the opportunity to be on *Shark Tank* and to give back to budding entrepreneurs.

Natalie, Dan, Andy, Will, Peter, Marshall, and Richard, you have all been great mentors for my legal education. Thank you for your years of support.

My *Shark Tank* entrepreneurs, you know who you are—you're the best!

Virgil and Kathy D—a special thanks for all you did for my spirit.

Thank you, Mom. I know you're still watching.

And to you, Dad, for all your support and dedication, from your "mini me."

I thank all the countless people who have been there, helping me throughout my journey. You know who you are!

NOTES

Chapter 1

3   **Thomas Edison for the phonograph:** Alex Knapp, "Nikola Tesla Wasn't God and Thomas Edison Wasn't the Devil," Forbes.com, May 18, 2012. http://www.forbes.com/sites/alexknapp/2012/05/18/nikola-tesla-wasnt-god-and-thomas-edison-wasnt-the-devil/

3   **Charles Greeley Abbot, who invented:** Application for Abbot Awards: www.ases.org/wp-content/uploads/2012/12/abbot_app-rvsd-2.docx

4   **Frank Epperson, inventor of the Popsicle:** Lemelson-MIT, "Inventor of the Week," August 2004. http://web.mit.edu/invent/iow/epperson.html

4   **"It's a very small percentage":** Author N/A, "Avoiding the Inventor's Lament," *Bloomberg Business Week*, November 9, 2005. http://www.businessweek.com/stories/2005-11-09/avoiding-the-inventors-lament

Chapter 2

25   **Mary Anderson invented windshield wipers:** Author N/A, "Mary Anderson: Inventor of Windshield Wipers," Famous Women Inventors. http://www.women-inventors.com/Mary-Anderson.asp.

Chapter 3

48   **Rather than cut shapes out of materials:** Jill Scharr, "The Future of 3D Printing Materials," *Tom's Guide*, September 27, 2013. http://www.tomsguide.com/us/maker-faire-shapeways-video,news-17610.html

48 **which is why another term:** Author N/A, "Three-D Printing Scales Up," *The Economist*, September 7, 2013. http://www.economist .com/news/technology-quarterly/21584447-digital-manufacturing -there-lot-hype-around-3d-printing-it-fast

Chapter 4

57 **Unrecycled paper comprises about 40 percent:** Jet Russell, "Recycling to Keep Paper Out of America's Landfills," Greenbusinesswatch.org, date n/a. http://greenbusinesswatch.org/blog/recycling -to-keep-paper-out-of-americas-landfills

69 **Apple's iPhone has 14 percent:** Simon Sage, "Apple Snags 14 percent mobile market share in U.S., Still Behind Samsung and LG," iMore.com, May 2, 2012. http://www.imore.com/apple-snags-14 -mobile-market-share-in-u-s-behind-samsung-and-lg

Chapter 5

93 **When he was interviewed for *Time*:** "Jeff Bezos: Bio: An Eye on the Future," *Time*, December 27, 1999. http://web.archive.org/ web/20000408032804/http://www.time.com/time/poy/bezos5.html

100 **Kickstarter was launched in 2009:** Chance Barnett, "Donation Based Crowdfunding Sites: Kickstarter vs. Indiegogo," *Forbes*, September 9, 2013. http://www.forbes.com/sites/chancebarnett/ 2013/09/09/donation-based-crowdfunding-sites-kickstarter-vs -indiegogo/

101 **Increasingly, however, Kickstarter is becoming:** Erik Sofge, "The Good, The Bad, and the Crowdfunded," *Wall Street Journal*, August 18, 2012. http://online.wsj.com/article/ SB10000872396390443991704577579190431157610.html

103 **such as the campaign to send:** Nick Sohr, "Crowdfunding Tips From Indiegogo and Fundable," MDBizNews, October 10. 2012. http://mdbiznews.choosemaryland.org/2012/10/10/crowdfunding -tips-from-indiegogo-and-fundable/

104 **Indiegogo projects only have about:** Chance Barnett, "Donation Based Crowdfunding Sites: Kickstarter vs. Indiegogo." Forbes.com, September 9, 2013. http://www.forbes.com/sites/ chancebarnett/2013/09/09/donation-based-crowdfunding-sites -kickstarter-vs-indiegogo/

104 **People have raised money:** Ben Schiller, "Crowd-funding For Everything Else: Pets, Health Care, College, You Name It," *Fast Company*, October 26, 2012. http://www.fastcoexist.com/1680780/crowd-funding-for-everything-else-pets-healthcare-college-you-name-it.

105 **Whereas the donations on sites like Kickstarter:** Will Schroter, "Crowdfunding: How Does Fundable Differ From Kickstarter?" Quora.com, June 2012. http://www.quora.com/Crowdfunding/How-does-Fundable-differ-from-Kickstarter

106 **In addition, Fundable brings together:** http://gigaom.com/2012/05/22/fundable-debuts-as-a-kickstarter-for-corporate-set/

110 **And indeed, *Shark Tank* and:** http://www.youtube.com/watch?v=2-4KoO4-xxA

111 **Kevin O'Leary says:** Alice Daniel, "Inside the Shark Tank," Success.com, date n/a. http://www.success.com/article/inside-the-shark-tank#sthash.Np34V3IY.dpuf

Chapter 6

122 **Filing for a provisional patent could:** http://www.uspto.gov/inventors/independent/eye/201302/Advice.jsp

123 **Some researchers estimate that:** Kate S. Gaudry, "The Lone Inventor: Low Success Rates and Common Errors Associated with Pro-Se Patent Applications," Plosone.org, March 21, 2012. http://www.plosone.org/article/info%3Adoi%2F10.1371%2Fjournal.pone.0033141

126 **there is usually a backlog:** Author n/a, "Timing of the First Action Office on the Merits," PatentlyO.com, November 7, 2012. http://www.patentlyo.com/patent/2012/11/timing-of-the-first-office-action-on-the-merits.html

Chapter 8

173 **Jordan Eisenberg, founder of UrgentRX:** Mark Cohen, "How UrgentRX Crashed the Party at the Cash Register," *New York Times*, August 7, 2013. http://www.nytimes.com/2013/08/08/business/smallbusiness/how-urgentrx-crashed-the-party-at-the-cash-register.html?_r=0.

Chapter 10

200 **Both QVC and HSN command:** http://online.wsj.com/article/
SB10001424052748703805004575606463489605440.html

201 **After airing on a TV shopping:** John Grossmann, "A High-End
Brand Tries a Different Sales Channel," *New York Times*, October 3, 2012. http://boss.blogs.nytimes.com/2012/10/03/a-high-end
-brand-tries-a-different-sales-channel/

204 **QVC is known for showing:** Albany Irvin, "QVC Sprouts is Born!"
QVC.com, March 12, 2012. http://community.qvc.com/blogs/for
-the-home-talk/topic/273982/qvc-sprouts-is-born.aspx;

Chapter 11

231 **As of the end of 2012:** Joanna Brenner, "Pew Internet: Social Networking," PewInternet.org, August 5, 2013. http://pewinternet.org/
Commentary/2012/March/Pew-Internet-Social-Networking-full
-detail.aspx

237 **People who raced to the locations:** Brandi Hitt, "Justin Timberlake's Hidden Albums Treasure Hunt Sends Fans on Finders
Keepers Frenzy," ABC.com, May 30, 2013. http://abcnews.go.com/
blogs/entertainment/2013/03/justin-timberlakes-hidden-albums
-treasure-hunt-sends-fans-on-finders-keepers-frenzy/

238 **But what really made the difference:** Ben Sisario, "The Timberlake Brand, Carried Along on a Media Storm," *New York Times*,
March 27, 2013. http://www.nytimes.com/2013/03/28/arts/music/
justin-timberlakes-20-20-experience-album.html?_r=1&.

ABOUT THE AUTHOR

LORI GREINER is one of the most prolific inventors of retail products. She's created more than 400 products and holds 120 U.S. and international patents. She stars as the "warm-blooded shark" on ABC's hit show *Shark Tank* and is a well-known celebrity personality on QVC-TV, where she has hosted her own show, *Clever & Unique Creations by Lori Greiner,* for more than fifteen years. Greiner's collection of cleverly designed products range from kitchen gadgets to travel bags to some of the most popular and unique organizers for all around the home. They are regularly featured in top magazines such as *Town & Country, O: The Oprah Magazine, InStyle, Woman's Day,* and *Family Circle.* She has also been profiled in *Financial Times, Success,* and *Entrepreneur.* Her Silver Safekeeper® Jewelry boxes were chosen as one of Oprah's Favorite Things.

ABOUT THE TYPE

This book was set in Transitional 521, a Bitstream version of Caledonia, designed by William A. Dwiggins in 1938. He describes the face as having "something of that simple, hard-working, feet-on-the-ground quality" as well as "liveliness of action. [...] quality is in the curves—the way they get away from the straight stems with a calligraphic flick, and in the nervous angle on the under side of the arches as they descend to the right."

INVENT IT, SELL IT, BANK IT!